Für die Menschen, die ihre Heimat und Liebsten verloren haben und die wir nicht vergessen dürfen.
For the people who lost their homeland and loved ones. May they not be forgotten.

Autor sämtlicher Texte und Fotos: André Widmer
Layout: Lea Scheuring und Tanja Jablanovic
Lektorat/Korrektorat: Andrea-Maria Streb
Übersetzung ins Englische: Grania Buckley
Korrektur Englisch: Levi O'Neil

Bildbearbeitung: Pascal Rohner
Druck: Schellenberg Druck AG (Pfäffikon ZH, Schweiz)
ISBN: 978-3-033-03809-7

Author and Photographer: André Widmer
Layout: Lea Scheuring and Tanja Jablanovic
Editing and proofreading: Andrea-Maria Streb
Translation into English: Grania Buckley
Proofreading English: Levi O'Neil

Image Editing: Pascal Rohner
Printing: Schellenberg Druck AG (Pfäffikon ZH, Switzerland)
ISBN: 978-3-033-03809-7

André Widmer

DER VERGESSENE KONFLIKT
Zwei Jahrzehnte nach dem Krieg um Bergkarabach

THE FORGOTTEN CONFLICT
Two Decades after the Nagorno-Karabakh War

LEGENDS

 Capitals

 Cities/Villages

Occupied territories outside Nagorno-Karabakh

Occupied territories belonging to Nagorno-Karabakh

Area:

Armenia	29 743 km²
Azerbaijan	88 600 km²
(incl. occupied territories	11 458 km²)

Population:

Armenia (2013)	3,04 mio.
Azerbaijan (2011)	9,11 mio.
(occupied territories 120 300 [2009])	

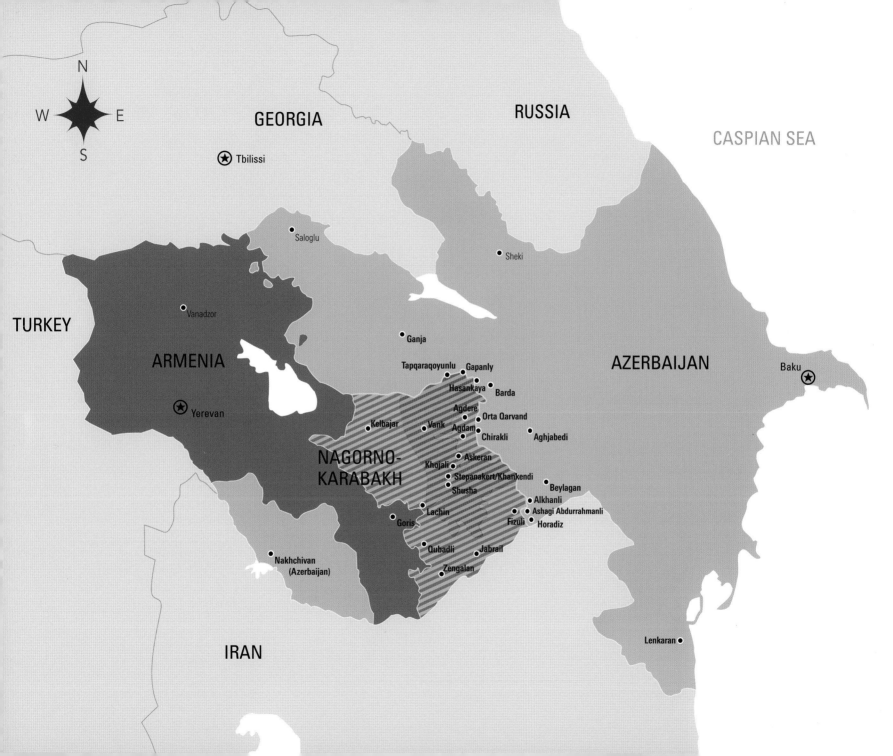

INHALT
CONTENTS

VORWORT

Der Zusammenbruch der Sowjetunion, der in den 80er-Jahren begann und in dem endgültigen Zerfall des Staates zu Beginn der 90er-Jahre gipfelte, war eine Zeitenwende. Der Eiserne Vorhang zwischen West- und Osteuropa fiel. Und auf dem Gebiet der ehemaligen Union der Sozialistischen Sowjetrepubliken (UdSSR) entstanden 15 neue Nationalstaaten. Doch der friedliche Wandel, den wir im Westen in Erinnerung haben, galt nicht für alle Teile der ehemaligen Sowjetunion. Mehrere Territorialkonflikte, die schon früher schwelten, brachen nun aus. So auch 1988 der Streit zwischen Armenien und Aserbaidschan um das in Aserbaidschan liegende Gebiet Bergkarabach. Von 1992 bis 1994 dauerte der daraus resultierende Krieg zwischen armenischen Separatisten mit Unterstützung der Republik Armenien und zerstreuten russischen Einheiten gegen die Republik Aserbaidschan. An dessen Ende stand die Besetzung Bergkarabachs und sieben weiterer Distrikte Aserbaidschans durch die Armenier. Um 30 000 Menschen starben. Der Konflikt brachte eine enorme ethnische Separation mit sich: 586 000 Aserbaidschaner wurden vor und während des Krieges aus den besetzten Gebieten vertrieben, weitere 250 000 aus Armenien. Aus den unbesetzten Regionen Aserbaidschans und Bergkarabachs flohen etwa 296 000 Armenier (laut US Comittee for Refugees, 1995). Die armenischen Separatisten führten in Bergkarabach und den weiteren benachbarten Provinzen Aserbaidschans ethnische Säuberungen durch. Vier UNO-Resolutionen verurteilten dies und verlangten den Rückzug der Okkupationstruppen, doch bis zum heutigen Tag befolgen die Armenier diese Forderung der internationalen Völkergemeinschaft nicht. Völkerrechtlich sind das besetzte Bergkarabach und die sieben Distrikte Kelbajar, Lachin, Kubatli, Jebrail, Zangelan, Agdam und Fizuli – zusammen fast ein Fünftel des Landes – weiterhin Teile Aserbaidschans. Die begangenen Kriegsverbrechen wurden bisher von keinem internationalen Strafgericht verhandelt.

Insbesondere in den einst zu mehr als 90 Prozent von Aserbaidschanern bewohnten Distrikten Lachin und Kelbajar wird von den Armeniern aber auch heute noch eine aktive Siedlungspolitik betrieben, was fundamental gegen Artikel 49 der vierten Genfer Konvention („Die Besetzungsmacht darf nicht Teile ihrer eigenen Zivilbevölkerung in das von ihr besetzte Gebiet deportieren oder umsiedeln") verstößt. Selbst der Bericht der OSZE-Mission in die besetzten Gebiete aus dem Jahre 2005 bestätigt, dass die Ansiedlungen von Armeniern in diesen Regionen erst nach dem Waffenstillstand stattfanden. Zwar wurden die Bergkarabach umgebenden Distrikte von den Besatzern als Pufferzone bezeichnet, doch illegale Siedlungstätigkeit und die Tatsache, dass das Separatistenregime der Bergkarabach-Armenier auch diese Gebiete als integralen Bestandteil seiner international nicht anerkannten „Nagorno Karabakh Republic" betrachtet, verdeutlichen das armenische Ansinnen: Es sollen so vollendete Tatsachen geschaffen werden. Zudem werden Ortschaften und Regionen von den Besatzern umbenannt oder nicht mehr in Landkarten aufgeführt.

Bei einem Besuch der zerstörten Stadt Agdam im März 2010 konnte ich mich mit eigenen Augen von einem weiteren Verstoß der Armenier gegen die Genfer Konvention überzeugen (Artikel 53: Es ist der Besetzungsmacht verboten, bewegliche oder unbewegliche Güter zu zerstören, die persönliches oder gemeinschaftliches Eigentum von Privatpersonen, Eigentum des Staates oder öffentlicher Körperschaften, sozialer oder genossenschaftlicher Organisationen sind (…)). In Agdam finden seit Jahren organisierte Plünderungen und damit verbundene Zerstörungen statt. Selbst ein Repräsentant des Besatzungsregimes hat diese Plünderungen mir gegenüber schriftlich bestätigt.

FOREWORD

The collapse of the Soviet Union, which began in the eighties and culminated in the conclusive disintegration of the union in the early nineties, was a historical turning point. The Iron Curtain dividing Western and Eastern Europe fell. And on the territory of the former Soviet Socialist Republics there emerged 15 new nation states. The peaceful transition that we in the West remember, however, does not hold true for every region of the former USSR. Various territorial disputes, smouldering for some time already, now erupted openly. Such was the case in the 1988 dispute between Armenia and Azerbaijan over Nagorno-Karabakh, a region lying within Azerbaijan's territory. The resulting war lasted from 1992 until 1994 and was fought between Armenian separatists, supported by the Republic of Armenia and scattered units of the Russian army, and the Republic of Azerbaijan. At its conclusion, Nagorno-Karabakh and a further seven districts stood under Armenian occupation. Approximately 30,000 people died. With the conflict came enormous ethnic separation: 586,000 Azerbaijanis were driven out of the occupied territories before and during the war, with another 250,000 expelled from Armenia. Some 296,000 Armenians fled the unoccupied regions of Azerbaijan and Nagorno-Karabakh (according to the US Committee for Refugees, 1995). The Armenian paramilitaries carried out an ethnic cleansing program in Nagorno-Karabakh and neighbouring Azerbaijan provinces. Four UN resolutions have condemned this and demanded that the occupying troops retreat, but as yet the Armenians have not complied with the international community's request. Under international law, occupied Nagorno-Karabakh and the seven districts of Kalbajar, Lachin, Qubadli, Jabrayil, Zangilan, Agdam and Fizuli – together comprising almost a fifth of the country – are still parts of Azerbaijan. The war crimes committed here have to date never been brought before an international court.

In the districts of Lachin and Kalbajar in particular, whose populations were once more than 90 per cent Azerbaijani, the Armenian occupiers are implementing an active settlement policy. This fundamentally contravenes Article 49 of the Fourth Geneva Convention ("The Occupying Force shall not deport or transfer parts of its own civilian population into the territory it occupies"). Even the report from the OSCE mission to the occupied areas in 2005 confirmed that the settlement of Armenians into this region took place only after the ceasefire. Though the districts surrounding Nagorno-Karabakh are designated by the occupiers as buffer zones, the Nagorno-Karabakh Armenians' separatist regime regards these areas as an integral part of its internationally unrecognised "Nagorno-Karabakh Republic". This, along with the illegal settlement activities makes the Armenians' intentions clear: it is to be presented as a fait accompli. Moreover, the occupiers have either renamed localities and regions or left them off maps altogether.

During a visit to the demolished city of Agdam in March 2010, I was able to satisfy myself first-hand of a further breach of the Geneva Convention on the part of the Armenians (Article 53: Any destruction by the Occupying Power of real or personal property belonging individually or collectively to private persons, or to the State, or to other public authorities, or to social or cooperative organizations, is prohibited [...]). In Agdam, organised looting and the destruction associated with it have been taking place for years. A representative of the occupying regime himself confirmed this looting to me in writing. Should the banished Azerbaijani populace ever return, it would be to find little remaining of its once blooming city.

Almost two decades after the end of armed hostilities, the Nagorno-Karabakh conflict has faded into obscurity with the general global public. This is the case despite the fact that no peace treaty exists

Sollte die zur Flucht gezwungene aserbaidschanische Bevölkerung jemals wieder zurückkehren, wird sie nur noch wenig von ihrer einst blühenden Stadt vorfinden.

Fast zwei Jahrzehnte nach dem Ende der kriegerischen Handlungen ist der Bergkarabach-Konflikt bei der breiten Weltöffentlichkeit in Vergessenheit geraten. Und dies, obwohl noch kein Friedensvertrag besteht und trotz Waffenstillstandsabkommen jährlich weiter Soldaten und Zivilisten ums Leben kommen. Die Suche nach Erklärungen und Gründen, nach Spuren und Meinungen ist für jeden, der sich mit dem Bergkarabach-Konflikt befasst, schwierig. Die Konfliktparteien suchen die Fehler beim Gegenüber. Der äußerst stark ausgeprägte Nationalismus auf beiden Seiten verstärkt die Unverrückbarkeit der Standpunkte und den Status quo in der Lösungssuche.

Als ich 2008 erstmals nach Bergkarabach reiste, war noch kein Buch geplant, sondern eine einzelne Reportage über die damalige Situation vor Ort. Mit der Recherche ein Jahr später in Aserbaidschan – also auf der anderen Seite dieses Konflikts – begann sich für mich ein Bild zusammenzufügen über die Kriegsfolgen in und um Bergkarabach. Ein Bild, das sich durch weitere Recherchen ergänzte. Es ist aber auch ein Bild, das niemand in seiner Gesamtheit voll zeichnen kann, weil jedes einzelne in diesem Konflikt erlittene Schicksal eine eigene Geschichte ist. Dieses Buch sollte deshalb als eine Sammlung von Momentaufnahmen aus einer instabilen Konfliktzone betrachtet werden. Die vorliegenden Reportagen, von denen einige in den letzten Jahren in diversen Zeitungen erschienen sind, konnte ich mit unveröffentlichten Informationen, Fotos und nach weiteren Recherchen ergänzen und detaillierter ausarbeiten. Bisher haben Historiker die Geschichte, Politikwissenschaftler die völkerrechtlichen Aspekte des Bergkarabach-Konflikts in vielen bisher erschienenen Publikationen eingehend behandelt. In diesem Buch sollen deshalb neben Fakten und Zahlen rund um den Konflikt vor allem die menschlichen Aspekte in den Fokus gerückt werden.

Zu den Recherchen: Im Frühling 2011 wurde mir ohne Angabe von Gründen auf dem Flughafen Eriwan (Armenien) das Visum verweigert, der Pass abgenommen und ich mit dem nächstmöglichen Flug nach Moskau ausgeschafft. So waren weitere Recherchen vor Ort in Bergkarabach nach 2010 nicht mehr möglich. Rückfragen des Schweizer Botschafters in Armenien ergaben, dass ich dort „persona non grata" bin. Auch der Botschafter erhielt keine Angaben über die Gründe vom armenischen Außenministerium. Ein erneutes Gesuch zur Einreise wurde 2012 abgelehnt. Ob der erschienene Artikel über die von den Separatisten zerstörte und geplünderte Stadt Agdam den Ausschlag dazu gab, bleibt im Dunkeln. Doch dass selbst einer Organisation wie der OSZE verboten wird, in nicht-militärischen Gebieten zu fotografieren, lässt aufhorchen. Es ist klar: Die armenischen Separatisten sind nicht daran interessiert, dass die gegenwärtige Situation einer breiten Öffentlichkeit zugänglich gemacht wird. Und diese besteht nicht nur aus renovierten armenischen Klöstern und Kirchen und einer schönen Landschaft, sondern auch aus zerstörten aserbaidschanischen Dörfern, Kultureinrichtungen, geplünderten Städten, beschädigten Moscheen und verlassenen Gegenden.

Verlierer dieses nach wie vor ungelösten Konflikts sind beide Seiten: Die Armenier, die den Krieg um Bergkarabach zwar militärisch gewonnen haben, aber aufgrund ihrer isolierten Lage wirtschaftlich keine wirkliche Perspektive haben. Und die Aserbaidschaner, die nach wie vor die Besetzung von fast 20 Prozent ihres Territoriums zu beklagen haben und deren Flüchtlinge bisher nicht in die Heimat zurückkehren konnten.

and that every year soldiers and civilians continue to lose their lives, ceasefire agreements notwithstanding. The search for causes and explanations, for clues and opinions, poses considerable difficulty for anyone attempting to investigate the Nagorno-Karabakh conflict. The opposing parties look for faults on the other side. The extreme nationalist sentiment – strongly pronounced on both sides – only serves to deepen the unwavering mindset of each people and entrench the status quo in the search for a solution.

When I first travelled to Nagorno-Karabakh in 2008 I planned on writing not a book, but rather a single report concerning the local situation at the time. A year later, during my research in Azerbaijan – that is to say on the other side of the conflict – a picture began to form before my eyes, of the consequences of the war in and around Nagorno-Karabakh. Further research brought to this picture more shape and definition. It is, however, a picture which no one person can describe in its entirety, as each individual element in this shared fate of war constitutes a story in itself. Consequently, this book should be seen as a collection of snapshots from an unstable conflict zone. Some of the present reports have appeared in various journals in recent years; these I have expanded and developed in detail after further research, now complemented with previously unpublished information and photos. Up until now, historians and political scientists have dealt extensively with the historical and international legal aspects of the Nagorno-Karabakh conflict in a number of publications. This book will, therefore, aside from presenting facts and figures relevant to the conflict, concentrate on bringing the human aspect into focus.

On the research: in spring 2011 at Yerevan airport (Armenia), I was denied a visa and my passport was confiscated, without any explanation. I was put on the earliest possible flight to Moscow and deported from the country. This made further on-site research in Nagorno-Karabakh after 2010 impossible. Queries addressed to the Swiss Embassy in Armenia yielded only the response that I was "persona non grata" there. Nor did the ambassador receive any particulars as to the reasons behind the Armenian foreign ministry's decision. A renewed attempt at entry in 2012 was also declined. Whether my article published on Agdam, a city destroyed and looted by separatists, was a deciding factor remains unknown. The fact, however, that even an organisation such as the OSCE is forbidden from taking photographs in non-military areas, must make us sit up and take notice. One thing is clear: the Armenian separatists have no interest in allowing visibility of the current situation to the public at large. This situation includes not only renovated Armenian monasteries and churches and a beautiful landscape, but also ruined Azerbaijani villages and cultural institutions, sacked cities, damaged mosques and abandoned districts.

Both sides are the losers in this yet unresolved conflict: the Armenians may have won the military war but because of their isolated position they have no real economic prospects, while the Azerbaijanis lament the occupation of almost 20 per cent of their national territory, the homeland to which their refugees have never been allowed to return.

UMKÄMPFTES BERGKARABACH

Im Laufe der Jahrhunderte gehörte das Gebiet des heutigen Bergkarabach wechselnd zu verschiedenen Großreichen. Anfang des 19. Jahrhunderts unterstellte sich als Folge des dritten russischpersischen Kriegs der regierende Khan von Karabach Russland. Unter der zaristischen Oberhoheit begann in Bergkarabach eine massive Ansiedlungswelle von Armeniern, aber auch Russen, Ukrainern und anderen Ethnien. Das Ziel bildete die Festigung der russischen Oberherrschaft mithilfe christlicher Bevölkerungen. Es ist allerdings auch nicht abwegig, dass vor und zu diesem Zeitpunkt bereits eine gewisse Anzahl von Armeniern in Bergkarabach ansässig war. Ab den 1830ern entwickelten sich in der Stadt Shusha, wirtschaftliches und kulturelles Zentrum Bergkarabachs, zwei Siedlungsteile: Das eine wurde von Muslimen bewohnt, das andere von den zugewanderten armenischen Christen. 1905 ereigneten sich im Zuge der über den Kaukasus verteilten Zusammenstöße zwischen Armeniern und Aserbaidschanern auch Gewalttätigkeiten in Shusha.

Nach dem Ende des russischen Zarenreiches und dem Zusammenbruch der nur kurz (1918) existierenden Transkaukasischen Demokratisch-Föderativen Republik (bestehend aus Georgien, Armenien und Aserbaidschan) erklärten sich die drei beteiligten Nationen für unabhängig. 1918 begann ein erster zwischenstaatlicher Krieg zwischen Armenien und Aserbaidschan um mehrere strittige Gebiete wie Bergkarabach, Nachitschewan und Zangesur. Nachdem die sowjetischen Bolschewiki in der Folge der Oktoberrevolution in beiden Ländern die Herrschaft einnahmen, bestimmten die Machthaber, dass Bergkarabach und Nachitschewan bei Aserbaidschan zu verbleiben haben und die einstige aserbaidschanische Provinz Zangesur der armenischen SSR anzugliedern sei. Der Beschluss, Bergkarabach bei der Aserbaidschanischen SSR zu belassen, wurde am 5.

Juli 1921 vom sogenannten „Kaukasus-Büro" der Sowjetunion unter Berücksichtigung historischer, geografischer und wirtschaftlicher Gemeinsamkeiten gefällt. Der armenische Nationalismus, der sich bereits Ende des 19. Jahrhunderts bemerkbar machte, begann sich im Nachzug der während der Wirren im zerfallenden Osmanischen Reich stattfindenden Deportationen zu radikalisieren. Die armenischen Todesopfer führten zu einem kollektiven Opferverständnis, das bis heute tief in der Volksseele verankert ist. Der Nationalismus bestand auch während der Sowjetzeit weiter. Viele Aserbaidschaner wurden dadurch damals zur Abwanderung aus ihrer Heimat Zangesur getrieben.

Ab 1975 trat die extreme armenische Terrororganisation Asala („Armenian Secret Army for the Liberation of Armenia") im Ausland in Aktion. Die vorwiegend aus Exilarmeniern bestehende gewalttätige Gruppe setzte sich dafür ein, ehemalige armenische Gebiete der heutigen Türkei zu „befreien". Anschläge in verschiedenen Ländern Europas und Nordamerikas forderten zahlreiche Opfer. Einer der damaligen Anführer, Monte Melkonian, starb später – 1993 – bei Kämpfen in Bergkarabach. Extremistische armenische Gruppierungen waren schließlich auch in Bombenanschläge in Aserbaidschan im Zusammenhang mit den Unabhängigkeitsbestrebungen der Armenier in Bergkarabach verwickelt.

Der zündende Funke

Mit dem im Zuge der erodierenden Sowjetmacht Ende der 80er-Jahre erstarkten Nationalstolz der Armenier können auch die ersten bewaffneten Auseinandersetzungen vor dem Beginn des Krieges um Bergkarabach erklärt werden. Der deutsche Politikwissenschaftler Heiko Langner macht als zündenden Funken für den Konflikt eine

CONTESTED NAGORNO-KARABAKH

Over the centuries, the area that is now Nagorno-Karabakh has had a chequered destiny, belonging alternately to various powers. Early in the 19th century, as a consequence of the third Russo-Persian War, the reigning Khan of Karabakh sought protection from Russia. Under tsarist sovereignty there began a massive wave of new settlement into the region, of primarily Armenians but also Russians, Ukrainians and other ethnicities. The aim was to consolidate Russian dominion by installing a Christian population. It is plausible, however, that a certain number of Armenians before and up until this time were already resident in Nagorno-Karabakh. From the 1830s onwards, the city of Shusha – the economic and cultural heart of Nagorno-Karabakh – developed with two distinct districts: one inhabited by Muslims, the other by immigrant Armenian Christians. In 1905, in the course of clashes between Armenians and Azerbaijanis through-out the Caucasus, Shusha too was host to outbreaks of violence.

After the fall of the Russian tsardom and the disintegration of the short-lived (1918) Transcaucasion Democratic Federative Republic (comprising Georgia, Armenia and Azerbaijan), the three participat-ing nations declared their independence. In 1918 began the first cross-national war between Armenia and Azerbaijan over a number of disputed regions such as Nagorno-Karabakh, Nakhchivan and Zangezur (Syunik). Following the October Revolution, the Soviet Bol-sheviks seized control of both countries and decreed that Nagorno-Karabakh and Nakhchivan were to remain with Azerbaijan, while the former Azerbaijani province of Zangezur was to be annexed to the Armenian SSR. The decision to leave Nagorno-Karabakh with Azerbaijan was made by the Soviet Union's so-called "Caucasus Bureau" on 5 July 1921, in due consideration of historical, geographi-cal and economic commonalities. The mass deportations, which took place during the turmoil of the Ottoman Empire's collapse, paved the way for Armenian nationalism – already noteworthy at the end of the 19th century – to become radicalised. The fatalities suffered by the Armenians led to a collective self-conception of victimhood, which to this day is deeply engrained in the psychology of the people. Arme-nian nationalism endured throughout the Soviet era and as a result, many Azerbaijanis were compelled to emigrate from their homeland Zangezur during this period.

As of 1975, the extreme Armenian terrorist organisation ASALA (the "Armenian Secret Army for the Liberation of Armenia") commenced its actions abroad. The militant group, composed primarily of exiled Armenians, was dedicated to " liberating" the former Armenian regions of present-day Turkey. Attacks in various European coun-tries and in North America claimed numerous victims. One of the ringleaders, Monte Melkonian, later died while fighting in Nagorno-Karabakh, in 1993. Extremist Armenian groups were eventually also involved in bomb attacks in Azerbaijan, in connection with the independence movement of the Armenians in Nagorno-Karabakh.

The igniting spark

As Soviet power eroded towards the end of the 1980s, Armenian nationalism grew stronger. This sense of national pride goes some way to explaining the first armed altercations before the start of the Nagorno-Karabakh War. The German political scientist Heiko Lang-ner identifies what is described as little more than a "trifle" as being the catalyst for the conflict; the Armenian residents of the Nagorno-Karabakh village Chardakli refused to accept an Azerbaijani as leader of a sovkhoz. This piece of news spread like wildfire, reaching as far

„Lappalie" aus: Im Dorf Tschardakli in Bergkarabach weigerten sich dort ansässige Armenier, einen Aserbaidschaner als Leiter einer Sowchose zu akzeptieren. Jene Nachricht hatte sich dann in Windeseile bis ins armenische Eriwan verbreitet, wo eine als Umweltprotest vorgesehene Massendemonstration der Opposition in eine Kundgebung zur „Wiedervereinigung mit Arzach" (Arzach ist die armenische Bezeichnung für Bergkarabach) mündete. Die ersten Todesopfer in Bergkarabach danach waren Aserbaidschaner. Schon 1987 gab es im armenischen Eriwan Bestrebungen mit dem Ziel, die bisher zur Aserbaidschanischen Sozialistischen Sowjetrepublik gehörende Autonome Region Bergkarabach der armenischen SSR anzugliedern. Am 20. Februar 1988 beschloss das armenisch geprägte Regionalparlament in Bergkarabach (zu jener Zeit lebten in der Region 73,5 Prozent Armenier und 25,3 Prozent Aserbaidschaner) den Anschluss an Armenien. Nach dem Beschluss und als Gerüchte vom Tod eines Aserbaidschaners die Runde machten, machten sich aserbaidschanische Zivilisten aus Agdam auf den Weg nach Stepanakert/Khankendi, um Antworten zu bekommen. Die Aserbaidschaner waren unbewaffnet (dies bestätigt die regierungsunabhängige aserbaidschanische Journalistin Aynur Elgunesh, deren Cousin 1988 jener Gruppe angehörte). Zwei Aserbaidschaner fanden schließlich bei Zusammenstößen mit ethnischen Armeniern am 22./23. Februar 1988 in Askeran den Tod.

Am 12. Juli 1988 erklärten die Armenier Bergkarabachs den Austritt aus der aserbaidschanischen SSR. Zwischenzeitlich übernahm zwar das sowjetische Innenministerium die Macht in der Bergregion. Doch ein Versuch der Sowjetkräfte, die Bergkarabach-Armenier im Mai 1991 zu entwaffnen, schlug fehl. Die Unabhängigkeitserklärungen Armeniens und Aserbaidschans 1991 und auch die einseitige Unabhängigkeitserklärung Bergkarabachs am 6. Januar 1992 ließen den Konflikt schließlich zum Krieg eskalieren. In Armenien wurden die Kommunisten von der Macht gefegt und eine eigene Armee auf die Beine gestellt. Derweil versank Aserbaidschan in innenpolitische Wirren und der Aufbau eigener Streitkräfte erfuhr eine entscheidende

Verzögerung. Armeniens Armee unterstützte nun die Separatisten der Bergkarabach-Armenier, welche begannen, die Bewohner ethnisch aserbaidschanisch geprägter Dörfer Bergkarabachs mit Waffengewalt zu vertreiben.

Im Herbst 1991 kam es dennoch beinahe zu einer friedlichen Einigung. Die Präsidenten Russlands und Kasachstans vermittelten eine Vereinbarung zur territorialen Integrität, des Nichteingreifens in interne Angelegenheiten und der Überwachung der Menschenrechte. Doch als am 20. November über Bergkarabach ein Helikopter mit einer hochrangigen Peacemaking-Gruppe, bestehend aus Russen, Kasachstanern und Aserbaidschanern, abgeschoßen wurde und die Armenier die Wiederaufnahme von Friedensgesprächen verweigerten, war eine weitere Eskalation die Folge. Zu Beginn des Jahres 1992 verstärkten die Armenier, auch mit Unterstützung versprengter Teile der russischen Armee des in der Region verbliebenen 366. Motorschützenregiments, ihre Angriffe auf ethnisch aserbaidschanische Siedlungen innerhalb Bergkarabachs. Traurige Berühmtheit erlangte dabei das Massaker am 25. und 26. Februar an der Bevölkerung des Dorfes Khojali bei Stepanakert/Khankendi, bei dem nach aserbaidschanischen Angaben 613 Zivilisten, davon viele Kinder und Frauen, ums Leben kamen. Der aktuelle armenische Präsident Serzh Sargsian, der zu jener Zeit als Kommandant in Bergkarabach kämpfte, wird im Buch „Black Garden" von Thomas de Waal folgendermaßen zitiert: „Vor Khojali dachten die Aserbaidschaner, dass die Armenier Menschen seien, welche nicht ihre Hand gegen Zivilisten erheben können. Wir waren fähig, diese 'Stereotype' zu brechen."

Am 8. Mai desselben Jahres fiel die aserbaidschanische Hochburg Shusha. Jener Sieg der Armenier bedeutete das Finale der ethnischen Säuberung in Bergkarabach. Ein paar Tage später gelang armenischen Einheiten auch die Eroberung der außerhalb des von ihnen beanspruchten Bergkarabachs gelegenen Region Lachin, die zu 99 Prozent ethnisch aserbaidschanisch besiedelt war und durch die die einzige Verbindungsstraße zwischen Armenien und Bergkarabach

as Yerevan in Armenia, where a mass demonstration planned by the opposition as an environmental protest morphed into a rally in favour of "Reunification with Artsakh" (Artsakh is the Armenian name for Nagorno-Karabakh). The first fatalities to follow in Nagorno-Karabakh were Azerbaijanis. By 1987 there were already efforts underway in Armenian Yerevan to annex to the Armenian SSR the Nagorno-Karabakh Autonomous Oblast, which belonged up to this point to the Azerbaijani Soviet Socialist Republic. On 20 February 1988, the Armenian-characterised regional parliament in Nagorno-Karabakh passed a resolution in favour of unification with Armenia (at the time, the region's population comprised 73.5 per cent Armenians and 25.3 percent Azerbaijanis). Following the resolution, as rumours circulated regarding the death of an Azerbaijani, Azeri civilians from Agdam set off on the road to Stepanakert/Khankendi to seek answers. The Azerbaijanis were unarmed; the non-government affiliated journalist Aynur Elgunesh, whose cousin was a member of this group in 1988, confirms this. Clashes with ethnic Armenians in Askeran on 22 and 23 February 1988 resulted in the deaths of two Azerbaijanis.

On 12 July 1988 the Nagorno-Karabakh Armenians declared their exit from the Azerbaijani SSR. In the meantime, the Soviet interior ministry took over control of the mountainous region. An attempt by Soviet forces in May 1991 to disarm the Nagorno-Karabakh Armenians was, however, unsuccessful. The declaration of independence from Armenia and Azerbaijan in 1991 and Nagorno-Karabakh's unilateral declaration of independence on 6 January 1992 led to an escalation of the conflict into open warfare. In Armenia, the Communists were swept from power and the country assembled its own national army. Meanwhile, Azerbaijan sank into domestic political turmoil and the formation of its armed forces suffered a crucial delay. The Armenian army then fell into step with the Nagorno-Karabakh-Armenian separatists, who began to drive out the inhabitants of ethnic Azerbaijani villages with armed force.

A peaceful settlement was nevertheless almost reached in autumn 1991. The presidents of Russia and Kazakhstan brokered an agreement on territorial integrity, non-intervention in internal affairs and the monitoring of human rights. Then on 20 November, a helicopter carrying a high-ranking peacemaking group composed of Russians, Kazakhs and Azerbaijanis was shot down over Nagorno-Karabakh. This, along with the Armenians' refusal to resume peace talks, resulted in a further escalation. Early in 1992 the Armenians, with the support of scattered sections of the Russian Army's 366th Motor Rifle Regiment, which had remained in the region, intensified their attacks on ethnic Azerbaijani settlements within Nagorno-Karabakh. Most notorious was the massacre of the population of Khojaly, a town near Stepanakert/Khankendi, on 25 and 26 February. According to Azerbaijani accounts 613 civilians were killed, including many women and children. Current Armenian president Serzh Sargsyan, who at the time fought as a commandant in Nagorno-Karabakh, was quoted in Thomas de Waal's book "Black Garden" as follows, "Before Khojaly, the Azerbaijanis thought that Armenians were people who could not raise their hands against civilians. We were able to break this 'stereotype'." On 8 May in the same year, the Azerbaijani stronghold of Shusha fell. This Armenian victory made way for the finale in the ethnic cleansing of Nagorno-Karabakh. A few days later, Armenian units succeeded in capturing Lachin, a 99 per cent Azerbaijani-inhabited region lying outside of Nagorno-Karabakh and thus outside the area to which they laid claim, but through which runs the only connecting road between Armenia and Nagorno-Karabakh. The Azerbaijanis were expelled from Lachin. A large-scale Azerbaijani counteroffensive brought only limited and short-lived successes. Within a few months, the Armenian separatists conquered the districts of Kalbajar, Agdam, Fizuli, Jabrayil, Qubadli and Zangilan – all of which lie outside Nagorno-Karabakh – and again drove out the Azerbaijani civilian populations. The Azerbaijanis managed nonetheless in 1993 and 1994 to free parts of the provinces Fizuli and Agdam. On 12 May 1994, a ceasefire agreement was finally signed. It is estimated that 25,000 to 30,000 people lost their lives to the war,

führt. Die Aserbaidschaner wurden aus Lachin vertrieben. Eine großangelegte aserbaidschanische Gegenoffensive führte nur zu kurzzeitigen Erfolgen. Der Reihe nach besetzten die armenischen Separatisten innerhalb weniger Monate auch die – ebenfalls außerhalb Bergkarabachs gelegenen – Distrikte Kelbajar, Agdam, Fizuli, Jebrail, Gubatli und Zangelan und vertrieben auch dort die aserbaidschanische Zivilbevölkerung. Immerhin gelang es den Aserbaidschanern noch, 1993 und 1994 Teile der Provinzen Fizuli und Agdam zu befreien.

Am 12. Mai 1994 wurde ein Waffenstillstandsabkommen unterzeichnet. Dem Krieg fielen schätzungsweise 25 000 bis 30 000 Menschen zum Opfer, 25 000 wurden verwundet. Aserbaidschan verzeichnet heute eine der höchsten Flüchtlingsquoten weltweit. Vermittlungsversuche der OSZE und von Russland organisierte Treffen haben bis zum heutigen Tag zu keinem Friedensvertrag geführt. Trotz des Abkommens von 1994 kommt es entlang der Waffenstillstandslinie zu Schießereien und Todesfällen.

with another 25,000 wounded. Azerbaijan now records one of the highest refugee rates in the world. Mediation attempts by the OSCE and meetings organised by Russia have not yet led to a peace treaty. Despite the accord of 1994, incidents of gunfire and fatalities continue to take place along the ceasefire line.

UNÜBERBRÜCKBARE DIFFERENZEN

Noch immer ist offen, wie es politisch weitergehen wird mit Bergkarabach und den weiteren armenisch besetzten Gebieten. In den zwei Jahrzehnten seit dem Waffenstillstandsabkommen hat man sich bisher nicht einmal auf eine Verhandlungsbasis einigen können – das Einzige, das von beiden Konfliktparteien festgehalten wurde, ist, dass man auf einen neuerlichen Waffengang verzichten wolle. Doch während die Armenier ihrerseits sich präventive Aktionen vorbehalten, schließt Aserbaidschan mittlerweile militärische Maßnahmen ebenfalls nicht aus. Nach wie vor ist aber die Diplomatie am Zuge. Die Organisation für Sicherheit und Zusammenarbeit in Europa (OSZE) versucht zu vermitteln. Bisher erfolglos. Stand der Dinge ist: Aserbaidschan bietet der Region Bergkarabach einen autonomen Status an. Dieser kommt für die armenische Seite jedoch nicht infrage. Die Angst vor Unterdrückung, wie sie die Armenier laut ihren Angaben zu erdulden gehabt hätten, seien zu groß, heißt es von armenischer Seite. Und so bleiben die Fronten nach wie vor verhärtet. Die Separatistenregierung Bergkarabachs ist von allen Verhadlungen ausgeschlossen. Die armenische Seite wird von der Republik Armenien vertreten.

Armenier aus Bergkarabach wollen an den Verhandlungstisch
Wie unverrückbar die Position der Bergkarabach-Armenier ist, zeigt ein Gesprächstermin mit dem Präsidenten der selbsternannten Republik bei meinem ersten Besuch in Bergkarabach (bis zum heutigen Tag hat sich an diesem Standpunkt nichts geändert). Hardliner Bako Sahakyan macht schnell klar, dass es keine Rückkehr zu Aserbaidschan geben könne: „Der damalige autonome Status war doch gerade der Auslöser des Konflikts", sagt er. „Es gibt kein Zurück in die Zeiten, wo wir extrem gelitten und die Besten unserer Nation ihr Leben verloren haben." Auf die Frage, wie groß die Gefahr

eines neuerlichen Krieges sei, antwortet er: „Man kann militärische Operationen nicht ausschließen." Doch, führt Sahakyan weiter aus, der Konflikt könne nicht mit Waffengewalt gelöst werden, weil dies sowohl in Aserbaidschan als auch in Bergkarabach viele Menschenleben fordern würde. „Für uns ist der einzige Weg der friedliche, durch Verhandlungen." Diese zeigten jedoch bisher keine Entwicklung, konstatiert Sahakyan. „Ich denke, dass wir bisher keinen Fortschritt erzielt haben, weil Bergkarabach über keine direkte Teilnahme an den Gesprächen verfügt." Die bilateralen Treffen Armeniens und Aserbaidschans zur Konfliktbeilegung begrüßt Sahakjian dennoch. Angesprochen auf die isolierte Lage seines selbsternannten Landes und ob sein 2007 vor den Wahlen formuliertes Ziel, die Einkommen verdoppeln zu können, realistisch sei, sagt er: „Die größte Garantie dafür ist unser Humankapital. Entscheidend ist nicht die Quantität, sondern die Qualität." Dies sei quasi der Antrieb der wirtschaftlichen Entwicklung. „Weil wir ein fruchtbares Land sind, ist zudem der Ausbau der Landwirtschaft ein substanzieller Bestandteil der wirtschaftlichen Entwicklung."

Auch für David Babayan, Pressesprecher Sahakjians, der beim Interview übersetzt, kommt ein Anschluss an Aserbaidschan nicht infrage. Der würde auch Armeniens Sicherheit gefährden, meint er: Kontrollierte Aserbaidschan die Wasserquellen Bergkarabachs, könnte es diese durch Verschmutzung gefährden. Aserbaidschan wiederum könne die Gebirgsprovinz außerdem gar nicht in die Unabhängigkeit entlassen, sagt der Regierungsbeamte. Im Vielvölkerstaat mit Aseris, Talyshen, Lesgier und Kurden würde dies Schule machen und das Land entlang der ethnischen Grenzen auseinanderbrechen lassen, vermutet Babayan.

IRRECONCILABLE DIFFERENCES

It is still unknown how political matters will develop in Nagorno-Karabakh and the other Armenian occupied regions. In the two decades since the ceasefire agreement, it has not been possible for the parties to agree on even a basis for negotiations. The only point firmly maintained by both sides in this conflict is that they do not wish to resume armed engagements. Yet while the Armenians for their part reserve the right to pre-emptive campaigns, Azerbaijan refuses likewise to rule out military measures. The next move is still for diplomacy to decide. The Organization for Security and Cooperation in Europe (OSCE) is attempting to arbitrate, to date unsuccessfully. The state of affairs is as follows: Azerbaijan has offered the Nagorno-Karabakh region self-governing status. For the Armenian side, however, this is not an option. The fear of oppression, which the Armenians say they have already had to suffer, is too great from their point of view. Thus the hardened fronts remain as immovable as before. The separatist government of Nagorno-Karabakh is excluded from all negotiations, with the Armenian side represented by the Republic of Armenia.

The Armenians of Nagorno-Karabakh want a place at the negotiating table

Just how unshakeable the Nagorno-Karabakh Armenians' position is was demonstrated in an interview with the president of the self-proclaimed republic, which took place during my first visit to Nagorno-Karabakh (and to the present this position remains unchanged). Hardliner Bako Sahakyan quickly makes it clear that there can be no return to a union with Azerbaijan. "The autonomous status we had then was what in fact triggered the conflict," he says. "There is no going back to the time in which we suffered so terribly, when the best of our people lost their lives." In answer to the question of how great the danger of a new war is, he answers, "We can not rule out military operations." But, Sahakyan goes on to explain, the conflict can not be solved by force of arms because it would claim many human lives, both in Azerbaijan and in Nagorno-Karabakh. "For us, the peaceful path is the only path, via negotiations." These, however, have not yet advanced in the slightest, states Sahakyan. "I think we have not achieved any progress up until now because Nagorno-Karabakh has no direct participation in the talks." He welcomes nonetheless the bilateral conflict resolution meetings between Armenia and Azerbaijan. When asked about the isolated position of his self-proclaimed country and whether his 1997 pre-election goal of doubling revenue is realistic, he says, "The best guarantee of it is our human capital. The deciding factor is quality, not quantity." This would effectively be the impetus behind economic development. "Since we have a fertile country, the development of agriculture, moreover, is a substantial part of our economic development."

David Babayan, Sahakyan's press officer and translator of this interview, is equally adamant that a connection to Azerbaijan is out of the question. This would also jeopardise Armenia's security, he says: if Azerbaijan were to control Nagorno-Karabakh's water sources, it could contaminate and endanger them. Azerbaijan on the other hand cannot simply grant the mountain province independence and release it, the government official acknowledges. In such a multiethnic country with Azeris, Talysh, Lezgian and Kurds, this would set a precedent and could cause the country to split apart along ethnic lines, Babayan speculates.

Some time after this visit to Stepanakert/Khankendi, Robert Avetisyan, a representative in Washington, reaffirmed this

Einige Zeit nach diesem Besuch in Stepanakert/Khankendi bekräftigt Robert Avetisyan, ein Repräsentant in Washington, abermals diese Positionen. Der Büroleiter bemängelt, dass seine Regierung von den Verhandlungen ausgeschlossen ist. „Das Format der Verhandlungen ist ineffektiv. Die Behörden Bergkarabachs haben immer wieder festgehalten, dass eine Lösung des Konflikts die Wiederherstellung des ganzen Verhandlungsformats benötigt. Bergkarabach muss unmittelbar an den Gesprächen teilnehmen", betont er. Und ergänzt, dass die von Aserbaidschan offerierte, „weltweit höchstmögliche Autonomie" und somit eine Rückkehr in die Republik Aserbaidschan nicht infrage komme. Während der 70 Jahre innerhalb des sowjetischen Aserbaidschans sei man diskriminiert worden. Und: „Die demografische Situation in Bergkarabach entwickelte sich schnell zum Vorteil der aserbaidschanischen Minderheit. Aserbaidschan war unfähig mit innenpolitischen Angelegenheiten in einer zivilisierten Art umzugehen. Der einzige Weg, unsere Identität im Land unserer Vorfahren zu behalten, war die Unabhängigkeit von der Regierung in Baku zu proklamieren."

„Die Geduld hat ein Ende"

Anlässlich meines ersten Besuches in Aserbaidschan 2009 findet ein Gespräch mit dem damaligen Pressesprecher des Außenministeriums und heutigen Botschafter Aserbaidschans in Südafrika, Elkhan Polukhov, statt. Wie auch bei weiteren Treffen in Baku erklärt er, dass Aserbaidschan den Armeniern in Bergkarabach den höchstmöglichen Autonomiestatus zugestehen wolle. Man sei bereit für weitere Verhandlungen, behalte sich aber das Recht vor, alle Mittel auszuschöpfen. Auch die militärischen. „Potenzial für die Diplomatie ist noch vorhanden. Aber wir werden kaum noch einmal 15 Jahre so weiter diskutieren", sagt er. Aserbaidschan fühlt sich von Armenien verschaukelt. Dies, weil jeweils bei Zusammenkünften festgelegte Verhandlungsprinzipien (die im Detail der Öffentlichkeit vorenthalten werden) im Nachgang wieder relativiert würden. Das Angebot Aserbaidschans an Armenien stehe. Nun gelte es für das Nachbarland, endlich auch einen Schritt zu machen, so Bakus Position.

Die Offerte Aserbaidschans an die Besatzer beinhaltet die höchstmögliche Autonomie für Bergkarabach innerhalb der aserbaidschanischen Republik. Analog der aserbaidschanischen Exklave Nachitschewan würde Bergkarabach ein regionales Parlament erhalten und könnte in Baku ein Verbindungsbüro betreiben. „Wir würden auch finanzielle Investitionen in Armenien selbst tätigen", sagt Polukhov. Voraussetzungen dafür sind zuerst der Rückzug der armenischen Truppen aus den besetzten Gebieten um Bergkarabach und die Wiedereröffnung aller Verkehrsverbindungen. Friedenstruppen der UNO oder der OSZE sollen danach die Rückkehr der aserbaidschanischen Flüchtlinge in ihre Heimat überwachen und ein friedliches Zusammenleben von Armeniern und Aserbaidschanern sichern. „Auch wenn wir verstehen, dass die Vermittler eine generelle Position einnehmen müssen: Wir wollen, dass die Mediatoren die Sache beim Namen nennen: Es ist eine Agression und Besatzung durch Armenien", stellt Elkhan Polukhov aber auch klar. Und: „Diese Region ist zu klein für sechs Nationen." Polukhov meint damit neben Georgien, Armenien und Aserbaidschan die umstrittenen georgischen Sezessionsgebiete Abchasien, Südossetien und auch Bergkarabach. „Wir können doch nicht die Büchse der Pandora öffnen." Und dann erzählt er eine Begebenheit, die weiten Kreisen kaum bekannt sein dürfte, aber aufgrund der geschlossenen Grenzen und der brüchigen Waffenruhe von großer Symbolkraft ist: 2007 und 2009 hat der in Moskau stationierte aserbaidschanische Botschafter von der aserbaidschanischen Seite her reisend Bergkarabach besucht und ist weiter nach Eriwan (Armenien) zu Gesprächen gefahren. Es mag ein symbolischer Schritt sein. Auch wenn sich sowohl Aserbaidschan als auch Armenien für eine friedliche Lösung ausgesprochen haben, ist eine Eskalation dieses nach wie vor ungelösten Konflikts trotz alledem nicht auszuschließen.

Bei einem weiteren Gespräch in der aserbaidschanischen Hauptstadt schildert Ramiz Nadjafov seine Sicht der Dinge. Nadjafov ist Generalmajor der Armee und im Verteidigungsministerium als Leiter für die internationale militärische Zusammenarbeit zuständig. Bereits

position once more. The diplomatic head criticises the exclusion of his government from negotiations. "The format of the negotiations is ineffective. Nagorno-Karabakh authorities have always maintained that a solution to the conflict requires restoration of the full negotiating format. Nagorno-Karabakh must participate directly in the talks," he emphasises. To this he adds that the Azerbaijani offer of "highest possible autonomy" in return for a reunion with the Republic of Azerbaijan is out of the question. In the 70 years as a part of Soviet Azerbaijan they were discriminated against. Furthermore, the demographic situation in Nagorno-Karabakh soon evolved to the advantage of the Azerbaijani minority. Azerbaijan was incapable of handling internal political matters in a civilised manner. "The only way to preserve our identity in the land of our forefathers was to declare our independence from the government in Baku."

"Patience has a limit"
During my first visit to Azerbaijan in 2009, an interview took place with the then press spokesman for the foreign ministry, Elkhan Polukhov, now Azerbaijan's ambassador to South Africa. As with other interviews in Baku, he makes it clear that Azerbaijan would be happy to grant the Armenians in Nagorno-Karabakh the highest autonomous status possible. While willing to engage in further negotiations, the Azerbaijani government reserves the right nonetheless to exhaust every means, military means included. "There is still potential for diplomacy, but we are hardly going to spend another 15 years going over the same discussion," he says. Azerbaijan feels it has been taken it for a ride by Armenia, because every time negotiating principles have been determined and fixed in meetings (the details of which have been withheld from the public), these have been subsequently qualified. Baku's position is that Azerbaijan's offer to Armenia stands, but it is time for the neighbouring land finally to take a step forward as well.

Azerbaijan's offer to the occupiers includes the highest possible autonomy for Nagorno-Karabakh within the Azerbaijan Republic.

As with the Azerbaijan exclave Nakhchivan, Nagorno-Karabakh would have its own regional parliament and could operate a liaison office in Baku. "We would even invest financially in Armenia," says Polukhov. The preconditions for this are, firstly, a retreat of Armenian troops from the occupied areas around Nagorno-Karabakh and the reopening of all transportation links. Peacekeeping troops from the UN or the OSCE should then oversee the return of the Azerbaijani refugees to their homeland and safeguard a peaceful coexistence between Armenians and Azerbaijanis. Polukhov also makes it plain, however, that, "Although we understand that the intermediaries must adopt a neutral stance, we want the mediators to call things as they are: this is aggression and occupation by Armenia." He continues, "This region is too small for six nations." By this, Polukhov means in addition to Georgia, Armenia and Azerbaijan, the disputed Georgian secessionist territories Abkhazia and South Ossetia, and Nagorno-Karabakh as well. "We simply can not open this Pandora's Box." Next he relates an incident that is probably not widely known but which, given the closed borders and fragile ceasefire, has great symbolic power: in 2007 and 2009, the Azerbaijani ambassador to Moscow visited Nagorno-Karabakh, travelling from the Azerbaijan side, and continued through to Yerevan (Armenia) for talks there. It may be a symbolic step. Although Azerbaijan and Armenia both expressed support for a peaceful solution in, a further escalation of this yet-unresolved conflict cannot, however, be ruled out.

In a later discussion in the Azerbaijani capital, Ramiz Nadjafov outlines his view of things. Nadjafov is a Major General in the army and has responsibility within the defence ministry as the director of international military cooperation. As early as 1994, the year of the ceasefire agreement with Armenia after the Nagorno-Karabakh war, the then president of Azerbaijan, Heydar Aliyev, signed a convention with NATO within the framework of the Partnership for Peace program. Nadjafov places emphasis on cooperation with the western military alliance, which has allowed Azerbaijan to modernise its armed forces. So far 1200 officers have completed NATO training.

1994, im Jahr des Waffenstillstandsabkommens mit Armenien nach dem Krieg um Bergkarabach, unterzeichnete der damalige aserbaidschanische Staatspräsident Heydar Aliyev den Vertrag für eine Zusammenarbeit mit der NATO im Rahmen des Programms Partnerschaft für den Frieden. Nadjafov betont die gute Kooperation mit dem westlichen Militärbündnis. Diese habe es Aserbaidschan erlaubt, seine Streitkräfte zu modernisieren. 1200 Offiziere hätten bisher eine NATO-Ausbildung absolviert. Derzeit stehen viele aserbaidschanische Soldaten an der etwa tausend Kilometer langen Grenze zwischen Armenien und Aserbaidschan; von der Grenze im Norden zu Georgien bis in den Süden zum Iran und entlang der Grenze der aserbaidschanischen Exklave Nachitschewan zu Armenien und entlang der Waffenstillstandslinie. Nadjafov: „Unsere Armee ist nicht mehr die von 1993. Wir haben neue Waffensysteme, sind stärker und in der Lage, diese Mission zu erfüllen." Mit „Mission" meint er die Befreiung von Bergkarabach und der anderen durch Armenien besetzten Provinzen Aserbaidschans. Seit fünfzehn Jahren werde nun im Rahmen der sogenannten Minsker Gruppe der OSZE der Bergkarabach-Konflikt erörtert – ohne konkrete Ergebnisse. Sein Land habe jedes Recht, seine territoriale Integrität wiederherzustellen. „Es gibt mehrere UNO-Resolutionen, die Armenien zum Verlassen dieser Gebiete auffordern. Doch der Druck der internationalen Gemeinschaft ist zu klein." Der Generalmajor betont zwar ausdrücklich, die diplomatischen Mittel seien noch nicht ausgeschöpft. „Aber wir verlieren langsam die Geduld."

Lachin-Korridor ein Knackpunkt

Die Region Lachin spielt in dem Konflikt eine entscheidende Rolle. Durch Lachin führt nach wie vor die wichtigste Hauptverkehrsachse nach Bergkarabach. Am 18. Mai 1992 nahmen die Armenier den aserbaidschanischen Distrikt ein. Sie bildeten auf diese Weise den sogenannten Lachin-Korridor. So konnte auch der Nachschub mit Waffen gesichert werden. Bei einem Gespräch mit dem stellvertretenden Außenminister und Vertreter Aserbaidschans in den Karabach-Verhandlungen, Araz Azimov, wird klar, dass der Korridor ein entscheidender Punkt bei den Verhandlungen ist. „Die Armenier verlangen, dass der Korridor in einer möglichst großen Breite unter ihrer alleinigen Kontrolle verbleibt", so Azimov. Araz Azimov ist schon seit vielen Jahren in die Verhandlungen involviert. Er erläutert den Rahmen des Lösungsvorschlags, mit dem Aserbaidschan einverstanden wäre: Der Rückzug der armenischen Paramilitärs könnte zunächst aus den ersten fünf Distrikten erfolgen und nach fünf Jahren schließlich aus Lachin und Kelbajar. Internationale Friedenstruppen sollten danach die Rückkehr der Flüchtlinge in ihre Heimat überwachen und ein friedliches Zusammenleben sichern. Dann erst würde der künftige Status Karabachs festgelegt. Und hier liegt denn auch ein weiteres Problem beziehungsweise sind die Verhandlungspositionen Armeniens und Aserbaidschans unvereinbar. Denn Armenien fordert vor allem, dass zuerst der Status Bergkarabachs festgelegt wird.

At present, a large number of Azerbaijani soldiers stand along the roughly thousand-kilometre-long frontier between Armenia and Azerbaijan, from the border with Georgia in the north to the Iranian border in the south, and all along the border with Armenia in the Azerbaijani exclave Nakhchivan and along the ceasefire line. Nadjafov cautions, "Our army is no longer that of 1993. We have new weapons systems, we are stronger and we are capable of fulfilling this mission." By "mission" he means the liberation of Nagorno-Karabakh and the other Azerbaijani provinces occupied by Armenia. For fifteen years, the body known as the OSCE Minsk Group has discussed the Nagorno-Karabakh conflict, without tangible results. He states his country has the right to restore its territorial integrity. "There have been multiple UN resolutions requesting the Armenians to leave the area, but the international pressure is too weak." The General distinctly stresses that diplomatic channels have not yet been exhausted, "but we are slowly losing patience."

The Lachin corridor: a sticking point

The region of Lachin plays a decisive role in the conflict. Through Lachin runs the most important primary traffic artery to Nagorno-Karabakh, as has always been the case. On 18 May 1992, the Armenians captured this district of Azerbaijan. In doing so they formed what is known as the Lachin corridor. This allowed them to secure their supply route with arms. In an interview with deputy foreign minister Araz Azimov, also Azerbaijan's representative in the Nagorno-Karabakh negotiations, it is made clear that the corridor is a crucial issue in proceedings. "The Armenians demand that they retain sole control of the corridor, with as great a width as possible," explains Azimov. Araz Azimov has already been involved in the negotiations for several years. He outlines the framework of the proposed solution to which Azerbaijan would be agreeable: the Armenian paramilitary could retreat initially from the first five districts and eventually, five years later, from Lachin and Kalbajar. International peacekeeping troops would subsequently oversee the return of refugees to their homelands and ensure a peaceful coexistence. Only then would the future status of Nagorno-Karabakh be determined. Herein lies a further problem, or more specifically an impasse making the negotiating positions of Azerbaijan and Armenia irreconcilable. This is because Armenia requires above all, that the status of Nagorno-Karabakh be established in the first instance.

01

BERGKARABACH
EINE ANNÄHERUNG

Zwischen den felsigen Hügeln, in der Talsohle, liegt in diesen Maitagen sattes Grün. Die Bäume haben ihre Frühlingsblüte hinter sich und tragen kräftiger werdende Blätter. Ein Flüsschen führt klares Wasser. Wer in den „Schwarzen Garten" will, muss hier vorbei. Wer in jenes fruchtbare Gebiet zwischen den trockenen Landschaften, den alpinen Hochebenen Armeniens und den kargen Flächen des zentralen Aserbaidschans möchte, muss die Brücke über das unscheinbare Flüsschen überqueren. Hinter der Brücke befindet sich ein Betonklotz, oval. Die Grenzstation. Links der Straße, am und vor dem Felsen, sind zwei Steinplatten mit christlichen Kreuzen platziert. Darüber weht eine Flagge, die derjenigen Armeniens frappant ähnlich sieht. Es sind Insignien der selbsternannten Republik Bergkarabach, die keine Nation der Welt bisher anerkannt hat. Der Weg in die sagenumwobene Region Bergkarabach, die völkerrechtlich zu Aserbaidschan gehört, führt nur mit dem Auto oder in einem Sammeltaxibus von Armenien her. Denn die Straßen- und Zugverbindungen nach Aserbaidschan sind seit fast 20 Jahren unterbrochen. Die militarisierte Frontlinie („line of contact") mit Schützengräben auf beiden Seiten verunmöglicht es, vom Mutterland Aserbaidschan her in dessen nun armenisch besetzte Gebiete zu gelangen. Das geht nur über diese Brücke hier im sogenannten Lachin-Korridor.

Auf der Fahrt zur Brücke und zur Grenze – einer Grenze, die eigentlich keine ist, weil in dieser Gegend wenig so ist, wie es sein sollte – ist zudem eine Hausruine zu sehen. Nur noch Grundmauern stehen, das Dach fehlt. Es ist menschenleer. Der erste Blick auf die besetzten Gebiete und Bergkarabach ist so die Sicht auf ein verlassenes Gebäude. Verlassen von den aserbaidschanischen Menschen, die früher hier lebten. 1992 mussten sie fliehen vor dem Krieg, vor den Armeniern. Der Lachin-Korridor ist mittlerweile kein Korridor mehr, weil die Sieger des Krieges um Bergkarabach nicht nur Bergkarabach, sondern auch weiteres aserbaidschanisches Land um diesen ehemaligen geografischen Flaschenhals eroberten. Die eigenartige Leere in dieser Landschaft wird man noch öfter antreffen. Es wird zudem auch schnell klar, wieso die Menschen dieses Land mit Bergkarabach, „gebirgige schwarze Garten", benannten. Denn die Nachbarregionen sind karg und trocken, Bergkarabach oben in den Bergen kann dank der hier verbreiteten Gewitter in den Sommermonaten mit fruchtbaren Feldern aufwarten. Die Wälder sind dunkelgrün und der leichte Wind streichelt die Wiesen. Bergkarabach ist wie ein gelobtes und gesegnetes Land, das zwischen Armenien und Aserbaidschan liegt. Doch all diese landschaftliche Schönheit kann nicht darüber hinwegtäuschen, was zu Beginn der 90er-Jahre geschah. Die Spuren des erbitterten Krieges sind nach wie vor sichtbar und die Folgen reichen bis in die heutige Zeit. Wer diesen schönen Flecken Erde verlassen musste, muss einen Schmerz des Verlusts in sich tragen, der kaum in Worte zu fassen ist.

01

AN APPROACH

Between the rocky hills, the valley floor in May is resplendent with luscious green. The trees have lost their spring blossoms and now bear hardier leaves. Clear water flows in a stream. Whosoever wishes to enter the 'Black Garden' must come through here. To reach that fertile land tucked between two dry landscapes – the alpine plateaux of Armenia and the barren flats of central Azerbaijan – one must first cross the bridge spanning this unremarkable stream. On the far side of the bridge is an oval-shaped concrete block; this is the border station. To the left of the road, in front of and on the rock, have been placed two stone slabs displaying Christian crosses. A flag that looks strikingly similar to Armenia's waves in the wind above. These are the insignia of the self-proclaimed Republic of Nagorno-Karabakh, as yet unrecognised by any nation in the world. The road to Nagorno-Karabakh, a region steeped in mystery, may only be travelled by car or shared taxi-bus departing from Armenia, though Nagorno-Kara-bakh rightfully belongs to Azerbaijan under international law. Roads and rail lines connecting it with Azerbaijan have been cut off for almost 20 years. The militarised line of demarcation, with trenches on either side, makes it impossible to access this now Armenian-occupied area from the motherland Azerbaijan. The only way is over this bridge in the so named Lachin corridor.

On the journey to the bridge and the border – a border that is in fact not a border, as in these parts little is what it ought to be – the ruins of a house can be seen. Only the foundation walls are still standing and the roof is gone. It is deserted. The first glimpses of the occupied territories and Nagorno-Karabakh are strangely reminiscent, akin to looking at an abandoned building. Abandoned, indeed, by the Azerbaijani people who once lived here and who were forced to flee from war and the Armenians in 1992. The Lachin corridor is by now a corridor no more, since the victors of the Nagorno-Karabakh War seized not only Nagorno-Karabakh but also additional Azerbaijani land surrounding the former geographic bottleneck. The peculiar emptiness of the countryside here is to be found again and again. It is also soon apparent why people have called this land Nagorno-Karabakh, meaning "mountainous black garden". The neighbouring regions are bare and dry, but up here in the mountains Nagorno-Karabakh is watered by storms over the summer months, which are to thank for its fertile fields. The woods are dark green and a light wind caresses the meadows. Nagorno-Karabakh is like a praised and blessed land lying between Armenia and Azerbaijan. Yet all this scenic beauty cannot disguise what took place at the beginning of the 1990s. The traces of a bitter war are still visible and its ramifica-tions persist to this day. Those compelled to leave this beautiful patch of earth must surely bear an aching sense of loss that can hardly be expressed in words.

02

BERGKARABACH
DER VERWUNDETE GARTEN

Die Moschee steht noch, wenngleich erheblich beschädigt. Viele Wohnblocks, die Brandspuren aufweisen und bei denen die Fensterscheiben fehlen, sind nur teilweise oder gar nicht bewohnt. Die Gebäude im Städtchen Shusha in Bergkarabach sind gezeichnet vom Krieg. Die Stimmung ist trist in der Ortschaft. Eine alte Frau bettelt um Almosen, jemand versucht, auf der Straße ein paar Beeren zu verkaufen. Doch Käufer sind rar. Vor dem Krieg bevölkerten die Stadt 15 000 Einwohner, die meisten von ihnen waren ethnische Aserbaidschaner und nur ein paar Hundert Armenier. Jetzt leben ausschließlich Armenier, vielleicht 3000 an der Zahl, hier.

Fremde Besucher fallen schnell auf; innert wenige Minuten erscheint ein zivil gekleideter Polizist und will die Ausweispapiere sehen. Wer in Bergkarabach umherreist, muss dem Außenministerium der selbsternannten Republik bei der Registrierung ganz genau deklarieren, welche Ortschaften er zu besuchen beabsichtigt. Orte wie die Geisterstadt Agdam sind offiziell Sperrgebiet, Shusha aber mit seiner nach dem Krieg renovierten armenischen Kirche ist frei zugänglich. Die Auseinandersetzung zwischen den muslimischen Aserbaidschanern und christlichen Armeniern in Bergkarabach war und ist aber nicht religiös motiviert, obwohl das Gebiet an einer Schnittstelle zwischen islamisch und christlich geprägten Regionen liegt. Vielmehr handelt es sich um einen ethnischen und territorialen Konflikt: Bergkarabach gehört nach armenischer Auffassung historisch zum eigenen Kulturkreis und wurde kurz vor dem Krieg zu mehr als drei Vierteln

von Armeniern bewohnt, liegt jedoch mitten in Aserbaidschan. Mittlerweile nutzen die Armenier jedoch die christliche Religion sehr stark zur Identitätsfindung und zur Untermauerung ihres Anspruches auf das besetzte Land. Viel Augenmerk wurde denn auch in Shusha auf den Bau und die Renovation der armenisch-orthodoxen Kirchen gelegt.

Zurück in Stepanakert/Khankendi, der Hauptstadt der nicht anerkannten Republik Bergkarabach. Die Azatamartikneri-Allee ist die zentrale Straße in der Kapitale und dementsprechend belebt. Sie ist gesäumt von kleinen und größeren, moderneren und einfacheren Gebäuden und Geschäften. Hier liegt in einem Hinterhof ein Busbahnhof. Es ist der Umschlagplatz, wo die Marschrutkas (Minibusse) und Taxis aus und nach Eriwan anhalten. Gefahren wird die stundenlange Strecke nach Armenien erst, wenn es sich für den Fahrer lohnt, das heißt, die Fahrzeuge mit Passagieren voll besetzt sind. Mit etwa 5000 Dram oder umgerechnet etwa 10 Euro ist der Fahrpreis mit dem Minibus spottbillig. Einige Leute bevorzugen dennoch die bequemere, schnellere, aber auch teurere Variante mit dem Taxi. „Wenn ein Mann mit einer Frau Sex haben will, die Frau aber nicht möchte und der Mann sie dazu zwingt, ist das ein Verbrechen", erläutert ein etwa fünfzigjähriger, großer Mann beim Taxistand seine Sicht des Konflikts. „So verhält es sich mit Bergkarabach, wir werden nie mehr mit den Aserbaidschanern zusammenleben können", sagt er. Der Mann ist Offizier der separatistischen Bergkarabach-Armee. Er fährt heute zurück zu seiner Familie, die in Armeniens Hauptstadt Eriwan lebt. Er ist nicht der Einzige, der in Bergkarabach Dienst tut, aber in Armenien zu Hause ist. Die Armee ist in dieser Gegend nicht nur der Sicherheitsgarant. Sie ist auch der wichtigste Arbeitgeber.

Eine Spur von Normalität
Anders als in anderen Ortschaften in Bergkarabach gibt es in Stepanakert/Khankendi seit dem Waffenstillstand von 1994 einen wirtschaftlichen Aufschwung. Es wurde viel gebaut. Spuren der

02

NAGORNO-KARABAKH
THE WOUNDED GARDEN

The mosque still stands, despite substantial damage. Many apartment buildings, showing scorch marks and lacking windowpanes, are only partly inhabited or not at all. The buildings of the town of Shusha in Nagorno-Karabakh have been scarred by war. The atmosphere of the place is gloomy. An old woman begs for alms, someone tries to sell berries on the street. But buyers are few and far between. Before the war, the city was home to 15,000 people, most of them ethnic Azerbaijanis with only a few hundred Armenians. Now there are only Armenians here, perhaps 3,000 in number.

Foreign visitors stand out and are quickly noticed; within a few minutes, a plainclothes policeman appears and asks to see identification papers. Anyone wanting to travel around Nagorno-Karabakh is required to draw up a specific list of places they intend to visit. These must be declared to the foreign ministry of the self-declared republic at the time of registration. Places such as the ghost town Agdam are officially restricted areas, but Shusha, with its post-war-renovated Armenian church, is freely accessible. The quarrel between Muslim Azerbaijanis and Christian Armenians in Nagorno-Karabakh, however, wasn't and isn't religiously motivated, though the area lies on a junction of Islamic and Christian dominated regions. Rather, it is an ethnic and territorial conflict. From Armenia's perspective, Nagorno-Karabakh belongs historically within its own cultural sphere; its population was more than three-quarters Armenian shortly before the war, yet it lies in the middle of Azerbaijan. At the same time, the

Armenians make heavy use of the Christian religion to define their identity and support their claim to the occupied land. Consequently, a great deal of emphasis was placed on the construction and restoration of the Armenian Orthodox church in Shusha.

Back in Stepanakert/Khankendi, the capital city of the unrecognised Nagorno-Karabakh Republic. Azatamartikneri Avenue is the main street in the capital and accordingly lively. It is lined with buildings and shops small and large, from the more modern to the more basic. Here in a rear courtyard is a coach terminal. It is the hub where the marshrutkas (minibuses) and taxis travelling to and from Yerevan pull up. The hours-long journey to Armenia will begin only once it is worth the driver's while, that is to say when the vehicle is full up with passengers. At about 5,000 drams or roughly 10 euro, the minibus fare is ridiculously cheap. Some people prefer, however, the faster, more comfortable yet more expensive ride in a taxi. A tall man of about fifty is standing by the taxi stand and offers his view of the conflict. "If a man wants to have sex with a woman and the woman doesn't want to, but the man forces her to anyway, it's a crime," he illustrates. "This is how it is with Nagorno-Karabakh. We will never again be able to live together with the Azerbaijanis". The man is an officer of the separatist Nagorno-Karabakh Army. Today he is going back to his family, who live in the Armenian capital Yerevan. He is certainly not the only soldier serving in Nagorno-Karabakh but calling Armenia home. In this area the army is not just the provider of security. It is also the largest employer.

A vestige of normality
In contrast to other places in Nagorno-Karabakh, Stepanakert/ Khankendi has enjoyed an economic upswing in the time since the ceasefire of 1994. A lot has been built. Traces of the violent confrontation are now hardly to be seen in this city of more than 40,000 inhabitants: at most, a few bullet holes in old buildings. "After the war, it looked like Sarajevo or Grozny here," says the officer, not without some pride in the gleaming new city centre. Yet just a short

kriegerischen Auseinandersetzungen sind in der Stadt mit ihren 40 000 Einwohnern kaum noch zu finden, höchstens ein paar Einschusslöcher an alten Gebäuden. „Hier sah es nach dem Krieg wie in Sarajevo oder Grosnyj aus", sagt der Offizier nicht ohne Stolz auf den neuen Glanz des Stadtzentrums. Aber schon ein wenig abseits der belebten Hauptstraße sieht es anders aus: Trostlose Hinterhöfe. Überwucherte Metallverschläge. Balkone, die bedrohlich über Gehwegen hängen. Und Leute, die gelangweilt aus den Fenstern schauen. Der bescheidene Aufschwung hin oder her: Dass sich viele Männer jeglichen Alters tagein, tagaus auf den Straßen Stepanakert/Khankendis die Zeit vertreiben, zeigt das Ausmaß der Arbeitslosigkeit. Die Behörden beziffern sie auf zehn Prozent, tatsächlich dürfte hier aber jeder Zweite ohne Job sein. Viele junge Männer müssen nach Beendigung der Schulausbildung in die Armee eintreten. Die Gesellschaft der selbsternannten Bergrepublik hat einen der höchsten Militarisierungsgrade der Welt.

Anders als weite Teile Armeniens ist die Vegetation in und um Bergkarabach grün. Sonnenschein und die Niederschläge machen das Land sehr fruchtbar. In erster Linie werden Weintrauben, Maulbeeren und Weizen angebaut, doch der Krieg hat dem ehemals bedeutenden Agrarsektor stark zugesetzt. Die Jahresproduktion von fast 160 000 Tonnen Weintrauben vor dem Krieg sank auf 3250 Tonnen (Stand 2008). Einen Exportschlager stellt der Maulbeerenschnaps „Tutowji" dar. Die „Artsakh Brandy Company" vertreibt noch weitere ausgezeichnete Branderzeugnisse. Dies ist aber nur eine der wenigen Erfolgsgeschichten. Viele Landstriche dürfen nicht genutzt werden, weil nach wie vor massenhaft Minen in den Böden liegen. Für die Milchverarbeitung fehlen Teile der Produktionskette. Gemüse und Früchte aus dem „schwarzen Garten" reichen trotz des fruchtbaren Bodens kaum für die eigene Grundversorgung aus; zum Teil müssen landwirtschaftliche Erzeugnisse aus Armenien angeliefert werden. So buhlen die Bergkarabach-Armenier um ausländische Investoren und werben mit tiefen Lohnkosten. Ein Monatslohn beträgt in Bergkarabach umgerechnet 45 Euro. Die Regierung verweist stolz auf Investitionen aus den USA, der Schweiz, Russland und Australien. Doch Recherchen nach den entsprechenden Unternehmen verlaufen im Sande. Und bei den wenigen überprüfbaren Fällen handelt es sich fast ausnahmslos um Unternehmer aus der armenischen Diaspora. Der mit fünfzehn Millionen US-Dollar größte Investor ist die Karabakh Telecom von Pierre Fattouch aus dem Libanon, wo eine große armenische Diaspora existiert. Die als Monopolistin agierende Firma ließ ein Mobilfunksystem installieren und will das veraltete Festnetz erneuern. Im Zentrum Stepanakert/Khankendis befindet sich ein Geschäft der Firma. Vorangetrieben werden auch die Gewinnung von Kupfer und Gold, Letzteres in einer Mine im Distrikt Kelbajar (besetztes Gebiet außerhalb Bergkarabach).

Der Tourismus hält sich trotz der landschaftlichen Reize der Region in Grenzen. Der ausländische Fremdenverkehr in Bergkarabach beschränkt sich in erster Linie auf Besuche von einzelnen Abenteurern oder von organisierten Gruppenreisen zum Kloster Gandzasar. Die lokalen Behörden haben in der Vergangenheit die Zahl von 4000 Touristen pro Jahr veröffentlicht. Reiseliteratur wie Lonely Planet weist darauf hin, dass das Verlassen von Straßen und Gehwegen aufgrund möglicher Minen und Blindgänger gefährlich ist. Wohl würde sich Bergkarabach für Wanderer und Mountainbiker geradezu ideal eignen, doch die beschriebenen Gefahren machen den Aufbau eines solchen Spezialtourismus derzeit unmöglich. Auch wenn der Besuch Bergkarabachs von ihnen nicht verhindert werden kann: Die Behörden Aserbaidschans warnen davor, die besetzten Gebiete zu besuchen. Wer mit dem Visum und dem Stempel der „Nagorno-Karabakh Republic" an einer Zollkontrolle Aserbaidschans erscheint, dem wird die Einreise nach Aserbaidschan in der Regel verwehrt. Sollte der Status Bergkarabachs je verbindlich festgelegt, die Verkehrswege in alle Richtungen geöffnet und das Land entmint werden, könnte der Tourismus für die Bergregion möglicherweise ein signifikanter Erwerbszweig werden.

distance away from the busy main street things look different. There are bleak back yards, overgrown metal sheds and balconies that hang threateningly over footpaths. And bored-looking people peering from the windows. Modest upturn aside, the fact that so many men of all ages while away the time on the streets of Stepanakert/Khankendi, day in, day out, demonstrates the scale of unemployment here. The authorities put the number at ten per cent but in reality it could well be every second person without a job. Many young men are obliged to join the army after completing their school education. The society of the self-proclaimed mountain republic has one of the highest rates of militarisation in the world.

Unlike large expanses of Armenia, the vegetation in and around Nagorno-Karabakh is green. Sunshine and rainfall make the land very fertile. Grapes, mulberries and wheat are the primary cultivations, but the once substantial agriculture sector was badly afflicted by the war. The pre-war annual output of grapes was nearly 160,000 tons; production has plummeted to 3,250 tons, going by 2008 figures. One star export is the mulberry brandy "Tutovka". The "Artsakh Brandy Company" markets other renowned brandy products as well. This is, however, one of only few success stories. Vast tracts of land cannot be cultivated at all, due to the massive number of landmines still lying hidden in the ground. The missing segments in the production chain hamper dairy processing. Despite the fertile land, fruit and vegetable production from the "black garden" is barely enough to cover the basic needs of the population; to some extent, agricultural produce must be imported from Armenia. The Nagorno-Karabakh Armenians, therefore, court foreign investors, promoting their low labour costs as an incentive: a monthly wage in Nagorno-Karabakh amounts to around 45 euro. The government refers proudly to investments from the United States, Switzerland, Russia and Australia, but inquiries made about the respective enterprises come to nothing. In the few cases which can be verified and confirmed, the businesses turn out to originate almost without exception from the Armenian Diaspora. The largest investor is Nagorno-Karabakh Telecom, with fifteen million US dollars. It belongs to Pierre Fattouch from Lebanon, where there is a large Armenian Diaspora. This company, which acts as a monopoly, has installed a mobile communications system and wants to renew the antiquated fixed-line network. A shop operated by the firm can be found in central Stepanakert/Khankendi. Other projects to be driven forward include the extraction of copper and gold, the latter taking place in a mine in the Kalbajar district, an occupied territory outside Nagorno-Karabakh.

Tourism remains limited, despite the regions's appealing landscape. Foreign tourism in Nagorno-Karabakh is limited for the main part to visits from individual adventurers and organised group tours to the Gandzasar monastery. In the past, local authorities have published figures of 4,000 tourists per year. Travel literature such as Lonely Planet makes readers aware that it is dangerous to stray from streets and paths because of the possible landmines and unexploded bombs. Though Nagorno-Karabakh would in fact be ideally suited to hikers and mountain bikers, the dangers described above make the development of this kind of special tourism impossible. In addition, the authorities of Azerbaijan caution against visiting Nagorno-Karabakh and even though they cannot prevent it, they do what they can to discourage it. Appearing at the Azerbaijani customs control with a visa and stamp from the "Nagorno-Karabakh Republic" is usually a recipe for being refused entry to Azerbaijan. If, however, the status of Nagorno-Karabakh should ever be firmly established, the transport routes opened up in every direction and the countryside demined, tourism in the mountain region could potentially become a significant industry.

Money from the Diaspora

At least as important as the investments in local industries and the limited tourism trade is and has been the financial capital provided by well-off Armenians living abroad. This money has funded the building of infrastructure and in particular, the connecting road leading to Armenia, which measures over 300 kilometres. This road runs

Das Geld der Diaspora

Mindestens so wichtig wie die Investitionen in lokales Gewerbe und den beschränkten Tourismus aber waren und sind die Finanzmittel der wohlhabenden Armenier im Ausland für den Bau der Infrastruktur und insbesondere der über 300 Kilometer langen Verbindungsstraße nach Armenien. Diese Straße führt durch den sogenannten Lachin-Korridor über Hochebenen und Pässe und ist in relativ gutem Zustand – abgesehen von den Schlaglöchern, die aber von den Fahrern gekonnt und in horrendem Tempo umkurvt werden. So dauert die Fahrt von der armenischen Hauptstadt Eriwan nach Bergkarabach sechs bis acht Stunden. Vereinzelt sind unterwegs Tanklastwagen mit iranischen Autokennzeichen zu sehen. Der Iran hat handfestes Interesse am Handel mit Armenien und Bergkarabach: Die 2005 in Betrieb genommene, von den USA mitfinanzierte Ölpipeline, die von der aserbaidschanischen Hauptstadt Baku zum türkischen Mittelmeerhafen Ceyhan führt, bedeutet Konkurrenz.

Eine Visite in Agdam, einer vor dem Krieg fast ausschließlich ethnisch aserbaidschanischen bewohnten und nun verlassenen Stadt, die etwa 20 Kilometer von Stepanakert/Khankendi entfernt liegt, soll nun folgen. Der Besuch des Sperrgebietes, das nicht zu Bergkarabach gehört, aber ebenfalls besetzt gehalten wird, ist aber nur mit einer Spezialbewilligung des Verteidigungsministeriums erlaubt. Der spontane Versuch zeitigt eine längere Wartezeit für den Bescheid in einem Wachthäuschen bei der Kaserne im Zentrum Stepanakert/Khankendis. Die Soldaten sind blutjung, wohl keine 20. Eine Verständigung ist aufgrund der Sprachprobleme nur ganz rudimentär möglich. Ein freundlicher junger Wehrdienstleister hat große Freude über eine Schweizer Banknote als Souvenir. Es sind junge Menschen, ja fast Kinder wie er, die bei einem Waffengang auf beiden Seiten wie Kanonenfutter ins Gefecht und den möglichen Tod geschickt würden.

Das Warten im Wachposten ist schließlich nicht von Erfolg gekrönt: Es wird keine Genehmigung zum Besuch Agdams erteilt. Nun folgt ein Versuch, mit einem Fahrer verbotenerweise dorthin zu gelangen. Der Kurztrip von Stepanakert/Khankendi her über Land zeigt: Je näher die Ortschaften an der Grenze zu Aserbaidschan liegen, desto verlassener sind sie. Von vielen Häusern stehen einzig die überwucherten Grundmauern; manche Dörfer sind nur noch zur Hälfte bewohnt. Ein verlassener Bahnhof ist zu sehen. Das Gerippe eines Autobusses steht davor. Außerhalb der Ortschaft Askeran steht ein Denkmal mit einem ausrangierten Panzer auf dem Sockel. Verwelkte Blumen schmücken das Monument, das Rohr des Panzers ist auf das nahe Agdam gerichtet. Hinter Agdam liegt heute die Demarkationslinie zu Aserbaidschan. In der Nähe informiert ein blaues Schild, dass hier die Organisation HALO Trust das Gelände entmint hat. Ein Stück vor Agdam – noch nicht einmal die Vororte sind erreicht – sagt Ararat, der Fahrer, plötzlich „Milizija!" und wendet den Wagen. Nun ist auch dieser Versuch gescheitert, in die Stadt zu kommen. Wohl der Reiz des Verbotenen lässt vereinzelte Bergkarabach-Besucher die Visite der Geisterstadt dennoch machen – Fotos im Internet zeugen davon.

Agdam ist vielleicht das beste Beispiel für die ethnischen Umwälzungen, die diese Region geprägt haben: Einst wohnten hier 50 000 Menschen, fast alle Aserbaidschaner. Jetzt ist die Stadt verlassen und wird von ein paar Soldaten kontrolliert. Auf manchen armenischen Landkarten ist Agdam schon gar nicht mehr eingezeichnet oder umbenannt. Zurück in Stepanakert/Khankendi: Wie sieht die Meinung in der armenischen Bevölkerung darüber aus, was mit Agdam einst geschehen soll? Der junge Sassoun Baghdassarian drückt sich so aus: „Eigentlich ist mit dem Status quo momentan allen gedient. Die Gemüter müssen sich zuerst beruhigen, denn noch sind die Wunden frisch. Vielleicht in fünfzig Jahren können die Aserbaidschaner Agdam wiederhaben."

through what is known as the Lachin corridor, over high plains and passes, and it is in relatively good condition apart from the potholes, which are however known to the drivers and skirted around at horrific speed. Even so, the journey from the Armenian capital Yerevan to Nagorno-Karabakh takes six to eight hours. The occasional fuel tanker displaying Iranian country code plates is to be seen. Iran has a vested interest in trade with Armenia and Nagorno-Karabakh; the oil pipeline running from the Azerbaijan capital Baku to the Mediterranean port Ceyhan in Turkey – co-financed by the US and in operation since 2005 – means competition.

A visit to Agdam is set to follow. This city, inhabited almost exclusively by ethnic Azerbaijanis before the war and now abandoned, lies about 20 kilometres from Stepanakert/Khankendi. The restricted area, although not a part of Nagorno-Karabakh, is still held under occupation and visitors are only permitted with special authorisation from the ministry of defence. The spontaneous attempt occasions an extended period of time spent in a guardhouse at the central Stepanakert/Khankendi barracks, waiting for the answer. The soldiers are very young, probably none of them 20. Because of the language issues, only very rudimentary communication is possible. A friendly young recruit doing military service delights in a Swiss banknote given as a souvenir. It is young people – indeed children almost – such as him that both sides would send as cannon fodder into battle and possible death in the event of an armed encounter.

The wait in the sentry post is ultimately unsuccessful; the permit to visit Agdam will not be granted. The next attempt involves hiring a driver to take me there illegally. The short overland trip from Stepanakert/Khankendi reveals that the closer villages lie to the border with Azerbaijan, the more deserted they are. Many houses have been reduced to ruins, with only the overgrown foundation walls left standing. Some villages are now only half inhabited. A derelict railway station can be seen; the shell of a bus stands out the front. Outside the town of Askeran is a monument with a decommissioned tank mounted atop the pedestal. It is adorned with withered flowers and the barrel of the tank's gun is pointed towards nearby Agdam. Beyond Agdam is the demarcation line with Azerbaijan. Nearby, a blue sign announces that the HALO Trust Organisation has cleared this area of mines. Some distance before Agdam – we haven't even reached the outskirts – our driver Ararat calls out "Militziya!" and turns the car around. Now this attempt to reach the city has failed too. It seems that the appeal of the forbidden inspires the occasional visitor to Nagorno-Karabakh to visit the ghost town nonetheless, as photos on the Internet testify.

Agdam is perhaps the best example of the ethnic upheaval that has characterised this region; 50,000 people once lived here, nearly all of them Azerbaijani. Today the city is deserted and policed by a few soldiers. On some Armenian maps Agdam is already either no longer marked at all or renamed. Back in Stepanakert/Khankendi: what is the view of the Armenian population as to Agdam's future? What do they think should be done? The young Sassoun Baghdassarian offers the following opinion. "For the time being, the status quo is actually to everyone's benefit. First of all, everyone's feelings need to cool down, because the wounds are still fresh. Perhaps in fifty years the Azerbaijanis can have Agdam back."

Gebäude Nr. 7 an der Vazirov-Straße, Shusha (Mai 2008)

Building No. 7 on Vazirov Street, Shusha (May 2008)

Gebäude der Lehrer und Ärzte (links), Minarett der Ashagi Govharagh Moschee (Mitte), Shusha (Mai 2008)

House of teachers and doctors (left), Ashagi Govhar Agha Mosque (middle), Shusha (May 2008)

Yukhary Govharagha Moschee,
Shusha (Mai 2008)

Yukhary Govharagha Moschee,
Shusha (May 2008)

Gebäude Nr. 5 eines früheren Sanatoriums,
Shusha (Mai 2008)

Building Nr. 5 of a former sanatorium,
Shusha (May 2008)

Gebäude Nr. 5 eines früheren Sanatoriums,
Shusha (Mai 2008)

Building Nr. 5 of a former sanatorium,
Shusha (May 2008)

Ehemaliges Wohngebäude,
Shusha (Mai 2008)

Former residential building,
Shusha (May 2008)

Russische Schule,
Shusha (Mai 2008)

Russian school,
Shusha (May 2008)

Teilweise bewohntes Gebäude,
Shusha (Mai 2008)

Partially inhabited residential building,
Shusha (May 2008)

Shusha (Mai 2008)

Shusha (May 2008)

Straßenszene vor Lebensmittelgeschäft,
Shusha (Mai 2008)

Street scene in front of a grocery store,
Shusha (May 2008)

M.A. Rasulzade-Straße in Richtung
Yukhary Govharagha Moschee,
Shusha (Mai 2008)

M.A. Rasulzade Street looking towards the
Yukhary Govharagha Mosque,
Shusha (May 2008)

Schulgebäude,
Shusha (Mai 2008)

School building,
Shusha (May 2008)

Gebäude Nr. 1 der Oberschule,
Shusha (Mai 2008)

Secondary school Nr. 1,
Shusha (May 2008)

*Panzer-Monument bei Shusha, das an die armenische
Eroberung der Stadt von 1992 erinnert
(Mai 2008)*

*Tank memorial near Shusha commemorating
the Armenian capture of the city in 1992
(May 2008)*

Shusha (Mai 2008)   *Shusha (May 2008)*

Straßenansicht,
Stepanakert/Khankendi
(Mai 2008)

Street view,
Stepanakert/Khankendi
(May 2008)

Frühere Bahnstation Stepanakert/Khandkendis (Mai 2008)
Former railway station of Stepanakert/Khankendi (May 2008)

Ruine in Askeran (Mai 2008)
Ruin in Askeran (May 2008)

Neue Schule in Vank/Vangli, finanziert von einem Unternehmer der armenischen Diaspora, Rayon Kelbajar (Mai 2008)

School building in Vank, financed by a businessman belonging to the Armenian Diaspora, Kalbajar Rayon (May 2008)

03

SPUREN IN SHUSHA

Mit dem Gehstock klopft der alte Mann an seine metallene Bein-
prothese. Für ein bisschen Geld möchte er den Weg weisen zum
Eingang des Minaretts auf der rechten Seite der „oberen" Moschee.
Es ist ein sonniger Frühlingstag in Shusha und es sind fast zwei Jahre
seit dem ersten Besuch hier vergangen. Die deckelartigen Dächer
der Minarette der „Yukhary Govharagha" sind inzwischen entfernt
worden. Am auffälligsten ist ein neues Metalldach über der Gebetshalle. Die Gebetshalle wurde vom Schutt geräumt und ist jetzt leer.

Die Bauarbeiten an der oberen Moschee wurden im 18. Jahrhundert
begonnen und 1865 beendet. Das Gebäude ist eines der Wahr-
zeichen Shushas und ein Zeitzeuge der aserbaidschanischen Geschichte dieser Stadt. Shusha war über lange Zeit die größte ethnisch
aserbaidschanisch bewohnte Gemeinde in Bergkarabach. Ungefähr
in der Mitte des 18. Jahrhunderts gegründet, stellte sie einen der
Hauptorte des Khanats Karabach dar. Shusha war öfter umkämpft,
wurde von Persien und später dem russischen Zarenreich angegrif-
fen. Vor dem Krieg um Bergkarabach in den 1990ern war Shusha der
Stolz Aserbaidschans. Die Stadt war Geburts- und Wohnort grosser
Künstler wie des Komponisten Uzeyir Hajybayov (1885–1948), des
Literaten Yusif Vazir Chamanzaminli (1887–1943) oder von Khan
Shushinski (1901–1979), der den aserbaidschanischen Mugham-
Gesang (ein meist hochstimmiger Gesang, der nicht aufgeschrieben
und mündlich von Generation zu Generation weitergegeben wird)
stark mitprägte. Kein Wunder also, dass Shusha bis vor dem Krieg

denn auch mit mehr als einem halben Dutzend Musikschulen und
über 20 Bibliotheken über zahlreiche kulturelle Einrichtungen
verfügte.

Vorsicht ist geboten beim Gang hinauf über die Wendeltreppe im
engen Minaretturm der oberen Moschee. Die Stufen sind voller
Geröll und es ist stockdunkel. Ein paar Schritte weiter dringt etwas
Licht in den Aufgang hinein: Durch ein Einschussloch ist ein Blick
auf die frühere Markthalle und ihre kriegsversehrte Umgebung
möglich. Oben auf dem Turm angekommen, bietet sich eine ein-
drückliche Aussicht auf Shusha. Es präsentiert sich heute wie ein
Flickenteppich: Zerstörte Gebäude in unmittelbarer Nachbarschaft
zu renovierten und bewohnten Gebäuden. Die einen Häuser mit,
die anderen ohne Dach. Geteerte und rudimentäre Straßen. Der
Krieg hat seine deutlichen Spuren hinterlassen. Während des Krieges
versuchten die Aserbaidschaner die drohende Niederlage gegen die
armenischen Separatisten von Shusha her abzuwenden und nahmen das nur elf Kilometer entfernte, von den Armeniern gehaltene
Stepanakert/Khankendi unter lang anhaltenden Granatenbeschuss.
60 000 Geschosse sollen auf Stepanakert/Khankendi niedergegangen
sein. Schlussendlich vergeblich. Denn das Bollwerk Shusha fiel
am 9. Mai 1992 und mit ihm das Schicksal der größten ethnisch
aserbaidschanischen Enklave in der ethnisch armenisch dominierten
Enklave Bergkarabach. Diese militärische Niederlage der Aserbaidschaner wird zuweilen als einer der größten Wendepunkte des
gesamten Waffengangs betrachtet. Nach dem Fall mussten, wie auch
aus anderen Siedlungen, aus Shusha die verbliebenen Soldaten und
Zivilisten mit Helikoptern ausgeflogen werden.

Kultureinrichtungen und religiöse Stätten sind beschädigt
Der Rundgang durch Shusha zeigt zwar, dass man in den letzten
Jahren etwas in die Infrastruktur investiert hat. Unter anderem ist
die ehemalige Markthalle renoviert worden. Einst fehlte auch ihr
das Dach, in der Zwischenzeit wurde der Mittelteil mit einer großen
Fensterfront versehen und das Gebäude erscheint kompakt. Doch die

03

TRACES IN SHUSHA

The old man taps his walking stick on the metal of his prosthetic leg. For a little money he is happy to show us the way to the entrance of the minaret on the right hand side of the "upper" mosque. It is a sunny spring day in Shusha and almost two years have gone by since my visit. The cap-like roofs of the "Yukhary Govharagha" mosque's minarets have by now been removed. Most notable is a new metal roof over the prayer hall. The prayer hall has been cleared of rubble and is now empty.

Construction of the upper mosque began in the 18th century and was eventually completed in 1865. The building is one of Shusha's landmarks and bears witness to the Azerbaijani history of this city. For a long time, Shusha was the largest ethnic Azerbaijani-populated town in Nagorno-Karabakh. Founded around the middle of the 18th century, it constituted one of the most important places of the Karabakh khanate. Shusha was fought over a number of times and was attacked by Persia and later the Russian Empire. Before the war of Nagorno-Karabakh in the 1990s, Shusha was the pride of Azerbaijan. The city was the birthplace and place of residence of important artists such as the composer Uzeyir Hajibeyov (1885–1948), writer Yusif Vazir Chamanzaminli (1887–1943) and Khan Shushinski (1901–1979), who strongly influenced Azerbaijani mugham singing (a generally highly harmonious singing tradition which is not recorded but passed orally from generation to generation). It is no wonder, then, that up until the time of the war Shusha boasted more than half a dozen music schools, over 20 libraries and a host of cultural institutions.

Care must be taken when going up the spiral staircase in the narrow minaret tower of the upper mosque. The steps are full of debris and it is pitch black. A few steps later, some light penetrates the dark of the stairway: a bullet hole affords a view of the former market hall and its war damaged surrounds. Reaching the top of the tower is rewarded with an impressive view over Shusha; it spreads out like a patchwork rug, with ruined buildings right next to renovated and inhabited buildings. Some houses have roofs, others are without and there are both paved roads and rudimentary streets. The war has clearly left its mark on Shusha. During the war, the Azerbaijanis used Shusha as a base in their attempt to stave off impending defeat at the hands of the Armenian separatists. Just eleven kilometres away, they took Armenian-held Stepanakert/Khankendi under sustained shelling and bombardment. It is estimated that 60,000 projectiles rained on Stepanakert/Khankendi. In the end to no avail, for the stronghold of Shusha itself fell on 9 May 1992, and with it was sealed the fate of the largest Azerbaijani enclave within the predominantly Armenian enclave Nagorno-Karabakh. This military defeat of the Azerbaijanis is regarded by some as the turning point of the entire war. After the fall, as with other defeated settlements, the remaining soldiers and civilians had to be flown out of Shusha by helicopter.

Cultural institutions and religious sites are damaged
A walk around Shusha shows, admittedly, that some investment in infrastructure has been made in recent years. Among other things, the former market hall has been renovated. Originally the roof was missing too. In the intervening years, the middle section of the market has been fitted out with a large window front and the building appears to be solid. Nevertheless, the town is still a long way away from a well-considered, integrated reconstruction. These are merely isolated measures. The will to rebuild is certainly there but the financial resources to do so are as lacking as ever in the isolated mountain

Ortschaft ist nach wie vor von einem durchdachten und ganzheitlichen Wiederaufbau entfernt. Es sind nur punktuelle Maßnahmen. Der Wille ist wohl da, aber es fehlen nach wie vor die finanziellen Ressourcen in der isolierten Region. Insbesondere die aserbaidschanischen Kultureinrichtungen, religiösen Stätten und Quartiere sind stark beschädigt oder zerstört worden und verkümmern unter der Besatzung. Imposante Gebäude wie das Gymnasium Nr. 2 fristen ein Dasein als Ruinen, denn aufgrund der geringen Bevölkerungszahl wird auch nur ein Teil der Infrastruktur benötigt. Einige Meter von diesem Schulbau entfernt befindet sich eine ehemalige Primarschule. Ein Holzvorbau erinnert an die Balkone in der Altstadt Bakus. Ein untrügliches Zeichen seiner Herkunft. Die Straße führt hoch zum Jydyr-Plateau, wo im Mittelalter Pferderennen stattgefunden haben sollen. In der Weite hinter dem Hügel sind die schneebedeckten Berge Bergkarabachs, das Massiv des 2725 Meter hohen Böyuk Kirs, zu sehen.

Der Spaziergang durch Shusha führt zur "Ashagi Govharagh"-Moschee, der unteren Moschee. Dieser Stadtteil ist arg in Mitleidenschaft gezogen. Die nahe gelegene Musikschule wurde bis auf eine Mauer komplett zerstört. Die im unteren Teil der Stadt gelegene Moschee ist ähnlich wie das weiter oben angesiedelte, große muslimische Gotteshaus trotz der Schäden erhalten, doch aufgeräumt wurde hier nicht. Der „Madrasah", einer vorgelagerten religiösen Schule, fehlt das Dach. Vom Haus hinter der Moschee ist nur noch eine Wand übrig. Auch von einem der Minarette hier ist der Überblick auf das stark beschädigte Shusha eindrücklich. In der Nähe befindet sich zudem das Gelände der pädagogisch-technischen Schule. Vom Gebäude selber allerdings gibt es nur noch Überreste. Ein paar Männer stehen beieinander, andere kauern auf dem Boden. Die Szenerie könnte nicht trostloser sein. In den zwei Jahren seit meinem ersten Besuch hat sich in Shusha abgesehen von wenigen baulichen Maßnahmen wenig geändert. Noch immer existiert eine unsägliche Perspektivlosigkeit inmitten der Erinnerungen an die besseren Tage dieser aserbaidschanischen Stadt.

region. In particular it is the Azerbaijani cultural establishments, religious sites and quarters of the city which are badly damaged or destroyed and which are left to decay under the occupation. Imposing buildings such as the Grammar School Number 2 languish as ruins, since the small number of citizens means only a part of the infrastructure is required. Some metres away from this school building is a former primary school. Its wooden porch is reminiscent of the balconies in the Old City quarters of Baku, an unmistakeable sign of its origin. The road leads up to Jidir Plain, where horse races are said to have been run in the Middle Ages. Looking into the vast expanse behind the hills, the snow-capped mountains of Nagorno-Karabakh can be seen, and rising above them, the 2725-metre high massif of Böyük Kirs Da ı.

Continuing the stroll through Shusha takes us in due course to the "Ashagi Govhar Agha" mosque, the "lower" mosque. This part of the city has been severely disfigured. But for one remaining wall, the nearby music school has been utterly destroyed. The mosque in the lower part of town resembles the larger one further up despite the damage sustained, but here no one has cleared out the rubble. The "Madrasah", a religious school situated in front of it, is missing its roof. Of the house behind the mosque, only one wall is left standing. From the minaret here, too, the view over heavily damaged Shusha makes a strong impression. In the same vicinity, the grounds of the pedagogical technical school can be found. There are but remnants to be seen of the building itself, however. A couple of men are standing around together while others crouch on the ground; the scenery could not be more desolate. The two years since my first visit have seen little change wrought in Shusha, a few construction measures aside. There is still the sense of hopelessness of a place without prospects, amid the memories of better days in this Azerbaijani town.

Sicht von der Musikschule zur Ashaghi Govharagha Moschee,
Shusha (März 2010)

View of the Ashagi Govhar Agha Mosque from the music school,
Shusha (March 2010)

Straße bei der Ashagi Govharagha Moschee,
Shusha (März 2010)

Street near the Ashagi Govhar Agha Mosque,
Shusha (March 2010)

Eingang und Hof der Ashaghi Govharagha Moschee,
Shusha (März 2010)

Entrance and courtyard of the Ashagi Govhar Agha Mosque,
Shusha (March 2010)

Blick vom Innenhof des Gebäudes Nr. 7 (Pioniere) an der Vazirov-Straße Richtung Ashagi Govharagha Moschee, Shusha (März 2010)

View from the courtyard of Building No. 7 (Pioneers' House) on Vazirov Street looking towards the Ashagi Govhar Agha Mosque, Shusha (March 2010)

Innenansicht Ashagi Govharagha Moschee,
Shusha (März 2010)

Inside the Ashagi Govhar Agha Mosque,
Shusha (March 2010)

Sicht von der Ashagi Govharagha Moschee Richtung Vazirov-Straße,
Shusha (März 2010)

View from the Ashagi Govhar Agha Mosque onto Vazirov Street,
Shusha (March 2010)

Sicht von der Ashagi Govharagha Moschee,
Shusha (März 2010)

View from the Ashagi Govhar Agha Mosque,
Shusha (March 2010)

Sicht von der Ashagi Govharagha Moschee,
Shusha (März 2010)

View from the Ashagi Govhar Agha Mosque,
Shusha (March 2010)

Früheres Gebäude des Komitees der kommunistischen Partei,
danach Musikschule,
Shusha (März 2010)

Former headquarters of the Communist Party's Regional Committee,
later a music school,
Shusha (March 2010)

Einschulungs-Gebäude Nr. 2,
Shusha (März 2010)

Boarding school No. 2,
Shusha (March 2010)

Gebäude und Schulhof der pädagogisch-technischen Schule,
Shusha (März 2010)

Building and schoolyard of the pedagogical technical school,
Shusha (March 2010)

Straßenszene bei der pädagogisch-technischen Schule, Shusha (März 2010)

Street view near the pedagogical technical school, Shusha (March 2010)

Ahmad Abbasgulu-Straße,
Shusha (März 2010)

Ahmad Abbasgulu street,
Shusha (March 2010)

Yukhary Govharagha Moschee,
Shusha (März 2010)

Yukhary Govharagha Mosque,
Shusha (March 2010)

Blick durch ein Einschussloch vom Innern eines Minaretts
der Yukhary Govharagha Moschee,
Shusha (März 2010)

View through a bullet hole from inside one of the minarets
of the Yukhary Govharagha Mosque,
Shusha (March 2010)

Gebäude Pionier-Camp bei der Jydyr (Pferderennen)-Hochebene, Shusha (März 2010)

Pioneer camp building near the Jidir (horse-racing) Plain, Shusha (March 2010)

Bank der Stadt Shusha (März 2010)

Shusha city bank (March 2010)

04

BERGKARABACH

AGDAM, DIE GEISTERSTADT

Ausgerechnet dort, wo kein Fremder etwas zu suchen hat, steht ein Schild mit der Aufschrift „bon voyage". Hier, ausgangs Askeran, einer Ortschaft im völkerrechtlich zu Aserbaidschan gehörenden, aber armenisch besetzten Gebiet, führt die Hauptstraße in unbesiedeltes Niemandsland. In militärisches Sperrgebiet. Auf der Fahrt von Stepanakert/Khankendi her geht es unter anderem vorbei an Militärbasen der Sezessionsarmee. In der Nähe der Straße befindet sich auch eine Übungspiste für Panzer. „Ich riskiere eine Verhaftung", hält Taxifahrer Robert demonstrativ fest. Doch für harte Dollars fährt er trotzdem nach Agdam. Dieses Mal soll der Besuch der Stadt gelingen – nicht wie beim ersten Besuch in Bergkarabach, als der Fahrer wieder umkehrte. Die Straße verzweigt sich. Ein Schild zeigt nach Tigranakert, einer Ausgrabungsstätte in der Nähe von Agdere. Die andere Straße führt nach Agdam. In der Ferne ist mittlerweile eine Eisenbahnbrücke auszumachen, kurz darauf ein muslimischer Friedhof. Die Ruhestätte ist verwahrlost. Hier hat schon lange niemand mehr nach dem Rechten geschaut. Das Gras wuchert, viele Grabsteine stehen nicht mehr aufrecht, andere liegen auf dem Boden. Die Verwandten der hier Begrabenen können diesen Ort der Stille nicht mehr besuchen oder pflegen. Sie sind getrennt von diesem Ort durch die ein paar Kilometer hinter Agdam befindliche Demarkationslinie. Nicht einmal das Recht, für einen Tag auf Besuch hierherzukommen, wurde geflohenen Aserbaidschanern von den Besatzern zugestanden.

Zerstört und geplündert

Das Taxi fährt weiter. Erste Außensiedlungen sind in der flachen Landschaft zu sehen. Dann ist die Stadt Agdam endlich erreicht – oder was von ihr übrig geblieben ist. Bis 1993 lebten hier noch gegen 50 000 Menschen – fast ausschließlich Aserbaidschaner. Heute ist Agdam verlassen, eine Geisterstadt – eine Folge des Kriegs. Topfeben ist die Region am Fuß zweier Hügelzüge. Die Bäume tragen noch wenige Blätter. Die frühlingshafte Vegetation erlaubt den Blick in die Ferne. Und dieser Blick ist ernüchternd: Ruinen, wohin das Auge reicht. Gebäude ohne Dächer. Häuserskelette, zerbröckelnde Grundmauern. Die Straßen sind längst nur noch Holperpisten. Agdam ist nicht nur verlassen, sondern auch zerstört und geplündert worden.

Es war der 23. Juli 1993, als Agdam nach lang anhaltendem Beschuss fiel und ihre aserbaidschanische Bevölkerung angesichts des bevorstehenden Vorrückens der Armenier floh. Die Einnahme wurde von der siegreichen Seite damit begründet, dass von hier aus die Aserbaidschaner mit Artillerie in Richtung Askeran und Stepanakert/Khankendi geschossen hätten. Denn strategisch günstig liegt Agdam; am Ende eines Tals. Nach der Eroberung folgte, was im Bergkarabach-Krieg offenbar Usus war: Häuser wurden angezündet, alles Brauchbare gestohlen. Die Organisation Human Rights Watch berichtet in ihrem Report aus dem Jahre 1994, der beide Seiten, aber mehrheitlich die Bergkarabach-Armenier für ihre während des Kriegs begangenen Kriegsverbrechen geißelt, von einer unnötigen Zerstörung Agdams nach der Einnahme. Ein OSZE-Vertreter äußerte sich laut dem Bericht von Human Rights Watch gar dahingehend, dass die Verwüstung der Stadt nicht das Resultat von Aktionen undisziplinierter Soldaten gewesen sei, sondern ein wohlorchestrierter Plan der sezessionistischen armenischen Führungsriege in Stepanakert/Khankendi vorgelegen haben muss.

Das Taxi fährt langsam durch die Ruinenlandschaft. In einer Straße ist ein jeepähnliches Gefährt zu sehen. Angst vor einer Kontrolle kommt auf – bloss nicht anhalten, die verdunkelten Fenster raufkurbeln. Gelegentlich durchqueren Agdam Fahrzeuge: So können Leute von einer

04

AGDAM, THE GHOST TOWN

Precisely here, of all places, right where no foreigner has any cause to be, stands a sign wishing everyone a "Bon voyage". It stands on the outskirts of Askeran; a village technically belonging to Azerbaijan but which in reality lies in an area occupied by Armenia. From this point the main road leads to the emptiness of no-man's-land within the military restricted zone. On the way here from Stepanakert/Khankendi we drove past many things, including the military bases of the secessionist army. Not far from the road there is also an excercise ground for tanks. "I am risking arrest," insists my taxi driver Robert, yet for hard currency he is prepared to take the risk and drive me to Agdam. This time I am determined to succeed in visiting the city, unlike my first attempt in Nagorno-Karabakh when the driver turned back. The road forks; one sign points the way to Tigranakert, an archaeological excavation site near Agdere, the other road leads to Agdam. By now I can make out a railway bridge in the distance and a little beyond it, a Muslim cemetery. This place of final rest is desolate; clearly nobody has seen to it in a long time. The grass is growing in abundance and many gravestones are crooked, while others lie on the ground. The relatives of those interred here can no longer visit or tend to the quiet burial grounds. The demarcation line that runs a few kilometres beyond Agdam separates them from it. The Azerbaijanis who fled this land are not granted even the right to visit the graveyard for one day.

Ruined and plundered

The taxi drives on and the first settlements in the flat landscape come into view. We have finally arrived at the city of Agdam, or rather at the site where what remains of it may be found. Up until 1993 almost 50,000 people lived here, almost all of them Azerbaijani. Today Agdam is deserted, a ghost town, a consequence of war. The region is completely flat and sits at the feet of two low-lying mountain ranges. There are but few leaves on the trees and the springtime foliage allows me to see well into the distance. The view is sobering: ruins as far as the eye can see, buildings without roofs, skeletal houses and crumbling foundation walls. The streets are little more than corrugated tracks. Agdam was not only deserted, but reduced to rubble and plundered as well.

The city fell on 23 July 1993, after a prolonged bombardment; the Azerbaijani population was forced to flee before the advancing Armenians. The victors justified the taking of Agdam as a response to artillery attacks on Askeran and Stepanakert/Khankendi supposedly originating from there. Indisputable is the fact that, positioned at the end of the valley, the city lay in a critical strategic location. Following the fall of the city, it was plundered, as seems to have been standard procedure during the Nagorno-Karabakh War: houses were set alight and anything of value was looted. The NGO Human Rights Watch in its report of 1994 castigates both sides, but primarily the Nagorno-Karabakh Armenians, for repeated war crimes committed during the course of the war. Equally condemned is the unnecessary destruction of Agdam following the city's capitulation. The same report cites a representative of the OSCE who opines that this destruction was not the result of a lack of discipline among the conquering troops, but more likely a well-orchestrated plan, carried out on the orders of secessionist commanders in Stepanakert/Khankendi.

The taxi drives slowly on through the devastated landscape. In one street we catch sight of a jeep-like vehicle and are seized with fear of an inspection; we mustn't stop, and winding down the dark tinted windows is just as inadvisable. Cars do pass through Agdam from time

armenischen Siedlung zur anderen gelangen. Diesen Anschein möchte Robert bewahren. Deshalb kommt auch ein Besuch des einzigen Gebäudes der Stadt mit im Krieg unversehrtem Dach, der Moschee, nicht infrage. Ein Blick aus der Ferne muss genügen. Wie ein Mahnmal ragt das muslimische Gotteshaus aus der Ruinenlandschaft empor, äußerlich verschont von den Brandschatzungen der armenischen Soldaten. Doch selbst jetzt, fast 20 Jahre nach Unterzeichnung des Waffenstillstandes, gehen die Plünderungen der Besatzer in Agdam weiter. Ein Metallhändler hat sich in der Stadt eingerichtet. Ein großes Areal ist mit gesammeltem Schrott übersät. Entlang der Straßen sind Gräben ausgehoben. Es wurden sogar die Wasserleitungen zur Weiterverwendung aus dem Boden entfernt. In einer Seitenstraße ist ein Baumaterialtransporter zu sehen; Backsteine sind ein weiteres, beliebtes Gut. Die Stadt Agdam ist verkommen zu einem einzigen Ersatzteillager für die Kriegsgewinner.

Die Regierung der Sezessionsrepublik unternimmt nichts gegen die systematische Plünderung Agdams. „Die militärische Aggression Aserbaidschans hat die gesamte Infrastruktur in Bergkarabach zerstört", so der armenische Repräsentant Bergkarabachs in Washington, Robert Avetisyan. Agdam habe aufgrund der dort befindlichen aserbaidschanischen Artillerieposten leiden müssen, dafür seien die Aserbaidschaner selber verantwortlich. „Das Einsammeln von Metall und Baumaterialien lässt sich durch den Wiederaufbau der armenischen Siedlungen in unserer Republik begründen, die schließlich von den Aserbaidschanern zerstört wurden", erklärt er. Diese von Privaten ausgeführten Aktionen seien nicht systematisch organisiert und extrem schlecht zu überwachen, meint Avetisyan weiter. Und schließlich betrachtet Bergkarabach diese einst als „Sicherheitsgürtel" besetzten aserbaidschanischen Provinzen mittlerweile als integralen Bestandteil seines Territoriums. Die latente Gefahr eines Beschusses aufgrund der Nähe zur Demarkationslinie hält die Armenier vermutlich auch davon ab, Agdam zu besiedeln.

Auch in anderen Teilen der besetzten Gebiete sind die Spuren des Krieges allgegenwärtig. Satellitenaufnahmen zeigen, dass insbesondere die Ortschaften und Städte im Ostteil der besetzten Gebiete – also zwischen Bergkarabach und der Waffenstillstandslinie – entvölkert

und größtenteils zerstört sind. Wie Agdam liegt Fizuli – Hauptstadt des gleichnamigen Rayons – bis auf ein Gebäude in Trümmern. Die von der OSZE im Jahre 2005 durchgeführte „Fact Finding Mission" bestätigt, dass in jener Region ebenfalls die Leitungen ausgegraben wurden. Fizuli, Jabrail, Agdam, einst bevölkerungsreiche Rayons Aserbaidschans in, denen nur ganz wenige Armenier lebten, sind praktisch menschenleere Gebiete geworden, die nur noch zur Plünderung und gegebenenfalls im Sommer saisonal als Weideland für Vieh dienen. Insbesondere in den zwischen Armenien und der sogenannten „Nagorno-Karabakh Republic" liegenden Rayons Lachin und Kelbajar wird aber entgegen den völkerrechtlichen Bestimmungen eine aktive Siedlungspolitik betrieben. Spärlich bewohnt sind zudem die Gebiete Kubatly und Zangelan, heißt es im OSZE-Bericht weiter. Namen von Ortschaften und Städten wurden von den armenischen Separatistenbehörden abgeändert, Bezirksgrenzen und Provinzen verschoben. Aserbaidschan sieht in diesem Vorgehen und der Zerstörung der Infrastruktur ein System und wirft den Besatzern vor, die Spuren der geschichtlichen Vergangenheit verwischen zu wollen. „Die Aktionen der armenischen Seite schädigen das kulturelle Erbe Aserbaidschans", sagt denn auch Elkhan Polukhov, Pressesprecher des aserbaidschanischen Außenministeriums, dazu. Zu 30 bis 35 Prozent sei die Stadt zerstört gewesen, als sie diese verlassen hätten, erzählen aserbaidschanische Flüchtlinge aus Agdam. Jetzt ist sie bis auf zwei Gebäude dem Erdboden gleich.

Langsam geht die Fahrt durch Agdam zu Ende. Ein einsamer Viehhirte treibt seine Herde mit Kühen, Schafen und Ziegen durch die Straßen der einstigen Stadt. Ein Autowrack, verrostete Fässer, Betonsäulen sind zu sehen. Das Brotmuseum (eines von nur zwei in der gesamten ehemaligen Sowjetunion) ist durch die beiden beschädigten Wandreliefs erkennbar. Das Dach fehlt; das Innere der einstigen Institution hat die Natur in Beschlag genommen, ein Baum wächst. Wie auch in anderen Teilen der Stadt, wo Ruinen und wuchernde Vegetation eine seltsame Symbiose ergeben. Agdam, des pulsierenden Lebens der Zivilisation, der kulturellen Güter und der Infrastruktur beraubt, ist zu einem einsamen, gespenstischen Ort im Niemandsland geworden.

to time, as people travel from one Armenian settlement to another, and this is the appearance Robert wishes to preserve. Given this, a visit to the mosque – the only building in the city which emerged from the war with an intact roof – is out of the question. I must make do with a glimpse of it from a distance. Like a monument, the Muslim house of God rises up from the landscape of ruins and towers over it, seemingly spared from the pillaging of the Armenian soldiers, at least on the outside. Yet even today, almost 20 years after the ceasefire was signed, the occupiers continue to loot Agdam. A metal dealer, for instance, has set up trade in the city and commands a large area strewn with assorted scrap metal. All along the streets trenches have been dug out; even the water pipes have been taken from the ground for reuse. In a side street we see a vehicle for transporting construction material; bricks too are prized items. The city of Agdam has been reduced to the state of a spare parts depot for the victors of the war. The government of the secessionist republic takes no measures to stop the systematic pillage of Agdam. "The military aggression of Azerbaijan has destroyed the entire infrastructure of Nagorno-Karabakh," declares Nagorno-Karabakh's Armenian representative in Washington, Robert Avetisyan. Agdam had to suffer because of the Azerbaijani artillery stations based there, therefore the Azerbaijanis themselves are to blame, he goes on to explain. "The collection of metal and building materials to rebuild Armenian settlements in our republic is warranted, as in the end it was the Azerbaijanis who demolished them." Besides, these activities are carried out by private persons, are not systematically organised and are extremely difficult to monitor, Avetisyan adds. And finally, these "safety margin" zones, as the occupying forces first described them, have now come to be seen as an integral part of their territory. The proximity of Agdam to the demarcation line and consequently the latent danger of coming under fire is presumably what has kept the Armenians from settling Agdam themselves.

In other parts of the occupied areas, too, signs of war are ever-present. Satellite images show that the villages and towns in the eastern part of the occupied area in particular – that is to say, those between Nagorno-Karabakh and the ceasefire line – are depopulated and to a great extent destroyed. Like Agdam, Fizuli – the main city in the rayon of the same name – lies in ruins, with just a single building left whole. The OSCE "Fact Finding Mission" conducted in 2005 confirmed that the water mains have been dug out in this region too. Fizuli, Jabrayil and Agdam, once heavily populated rayons of Azerbaijan in which few Armenians lived, have now become areas practically devoid of people, used only for looting and if necessary in summer, as a seasonal pastureland for cattle. In the rayons of Lachin and Kalbajar, on the other hand, which lie between Armenia and the so-called "Nagorno Karabakh Republic", an active settlement policy is in place, in defiance of the provisions of international law. In addition, the regions Qubadli and Zangilan are only sparsely populated, the OSCE report continues. The Armenian separatist authorities have altered the names of villages and towns, and shifted district boundaries and provinces. Azerbaijan identifies a systematic approach in these procedures and in the destruction of infrastructure, and has accused the occupiers of wanting to obliterate the historic record. "The actions of the Armenian side are damaging Azerbaijan's cultural heritage," laments the press spokesman of Azerbaijan's foreign ministry, Elkhan Polukhov, on the subject. Ethnic Azerbaijani refugees from Agdam report that between 30 and 35 per cent of the city had been demolished at the time they abandoned it. Now all but two buildings have been razed to the ground.

The drive through Agdam slowly draws to a close. A lone herdsman drives his assorted cows, sheep and goats through the streets of the one-time city. The wreck of a car, rusted drums and concrete pillars complete the scene of dilapidation. The Bread Museum (one of only two in the whole of the former Soviet Union) is still recognisable thanks to two wall reliefs, damaged though they are. Inside, the roof is missing and a tree is growing; the interior of the former institution has been commandeered by nature. As in other parts of the city, vegetation proliferates amongst the ruins, giving rise to a peculiar symbiosis. Agdam, robbed of the pulsating life of civilisation, of cultural assets and of infrastructure, has become a lonely, eerie place in no-mans-land.

Stadtrand Agdam
(März 2010)

Outskirts of Agdam city
(March 2010)

Agdam
(März 2010)

Agdam
(March 2010)

Selbst Leitungen wurden von den armenischen Plünderern aus dem Boden geholt, Agdam (März 2010)

Street where Armenian looters have taken even the water pipes from the ground, Agdam (March 2010)

Straße Suleyman Sani Axundov,
Agdam (März 2010)

Suleyman Sani Axundov Street,
Agdam (March 2010)

Straße in Richtung Moschee,   *Street leading towards the Agdam Mosque*
Agdam (März 2010)   *(March 2010)*

Garten der Pioniere mit dem dreiteiligen Denkmal der Freundschaft der drei kaukasischen Republiken Aserbaidschan, Georgien und Armenien, Agdam (März 2010)

Pioneers' Garden and the tripartite monument to the friendship of the three Caucasus republics Azerbaijan, Georgia and Armenia, Agdam (March 2010)

Garten der Pioniere,
Agdam (März 2010)

Pioneers' Garden,
Agdam (March 2010)

Brotmuseum, Agdam (März 2010)

Bread museum, Agdam (March 2010)

Agdam (März 2010)

Agdam (March 2010)

Beim Denkmal der Wehrdienstleistenden im 2. Weltkrieg aus Agdam
(März 2010)

Near the momument for the World War II combatants from Agdam
(March 2010)

Agdam (März 2010)   *Agdam (March 2010)*

Agdam (März 2010)   *Agdam (March 2010)*

Agdam (März 2010)

Agdam (March 2010)

Agdam (März 2010) *Agdam (March 2010)*

Denkmal der Wehrdienstleistenden im 2. Weltkrieg aus Agdam (März 2010)

Monument for the World War II combatants from Agdam (March 2010)

05

DIE GESTRANDETEN

„Man gab uns Steine, die Häuser bauten wir selbst". Das war im Jahr 1995. An der Verbindungsstraße zwischen den Städten Beylagan und Aghdjabedi lebt Chingis Huseyn Huseynov, der das erzählt, heute immer noch. Holz, Lehm, Tücher: Es ist eine ärmliche Behausung, in der er mit seiner Familie wohnt. Aus den Augen der Menschen hier ist ihr Schicksal zu erahnen. Huseynov kann sich noch genau an das Datum der Flucht erinnern: es war der 23. August 1993. Er und seine Familie leben heute im Exil von landwirtschaftlicher Selbstversorgung. Seit im Jahre 2009 hier einige Familien wegzogen, hat es vor Ort keine Schule mehr und die Kinder müssen abgeholt werden. Immerhin gibt es etwas staatliche Unterstützung. Ein bisschen Geld für Brot. Und die Flüchtlinge müssen keine Steuern zahlen. Auch Chingis Huseyn Huseynov möchte nichts anderes als wieder in seine alte Heimat zurück. „Mit der Hilfe Gottes werden wir zurückgehen."

In der Region Agdjabedi haben viele Flüchtlinge ebenso wie Huseynov längst noch nicht alle eine neue Unterkunft beziehen können. Eine staubige Piste etwas außerhalb der neuen Flüchtlingssiedlung Lachin (auch hier der Name der alten Heimat) führt vorbei an einem im Bau befindlichen Wohngebiet. In Sichtweite der Baustelle leben jedoch nach wie vor viele Familien unter menschen-unwürdigen Bedingungen. Ihre Behausungen sind notdürftig aus Abdeckplatten, Lehm und Holz zusammengezimmert. Einige Dächer sind mit Erde belegt. Immerhin versorgt eine Stromleitung die Gegend. Hier wohnt

auch Asgar Bagitov mit seiner Familie, drei Generationen. Er führt die Besucher in den Raum, der unter der Erde liegt. Die Wände sind ausstaffiert mit Tüchern, der Boden mit Teppichen bedeckt. Die Decke wird mit einem mit Plastikfolie verkleideten Baumstamm gestützt. Seit 1992 leben die Bagitovs hier nun schon. „Unsere Lebensumstände in der Heimat waren viel besser. Wir hatten Wasser vor dem Haus, jetzt muss ich bis zu vier Kilometer gehen, um an ein Wasserloch zu kommen", erzählt Asgar Bagitov. Er ist der Regierung zwar für das Wenige an Unterstützung dankbar, hofft aber, dass sich die Situation, in der sich seine vielköpfige Familie befindet, bald bessert. In sechs Monaten sollen die Bagitovs ein neues Haus bekommen – jetzt erst, fast 20 Jahre nach der Flucht. „Doch eigentlich brauchen wir kein neues Haus, sondern wollen unser altes Land zurück", sagt Asgar Bagitov. Neben der fehlenden Wasserversorgung ist in dieser Gegend, in der die Flüchtlinge gestrandet sind, vieles anders als in der alten Heimat: Statt in einem fruchtbaren Tal wie in Lachin leben sie in einer kargen Tiefebene.

Ähnlich geht es zwei Frauen, die uns auf der ungeteerten Straße nebenan entgegenkommen. Die Namen der Frauen sind Malahat Maseieva und Fatma Dunjamaljeva. Auch sie leben hier von selbstversorgender Landwirtschaft und 15 Manat (etwa 12 Euro) monatlich und sollen auch ein neues Haus bekommen. Doch eigentlich möchten sie nur zurück in ihre alte Heimat, nach Vagazin, ein Dorf etwa 50 Kilometer nördlich der Stadt Lachin. Bitter sind die Erinnerungen an die Flucht im Jahre 1992. Vater und Bruder wurden als Geiseln genommen und folgten ihnen erst nach zwei Jahren. Einer sei geflüchtet, der andere im Austausch. Die Frauen erzählen von der eigenen Flucht: Bereits zu Beginn wurden den Flüchtlingen die mitgeführten Schafe, Kleider und Schuhe geraubt. Unterwegs ernährte man sich von Wildpflanzen. Nach drei Wochen Fußmarsch hatten sie Aghdjabedi erreicht. Geblieben ist den Frauen wie vielen anderen die Sehnsucht nach den besetzten Heimatdörfern. Dörfern, die heute zum größten Teil in Trümmern liegen.

05

AZERBAIJAN

STRANDED

"We were given stones; the houses we built ourselves." That was in 1995. Chingis Huseyn Huseynov, who is telling me this, is today still living by the road connecting the towns Beylagan and Agdjabedi. Made of wood, clay and pieces of cloth, the house in which he and his family live is a humble dwelling. Seen from the eyes of the local people, his story is easy to guess. Huseynov can remember the exact date of their flight: it was 23 August 1993. He and his family now live in exile, eking out an existence as self-sufficient farmers. Since some families moved away from the area in 2009, the local school is no more and the children must be picked up and taken elsewhere. There is at least some support from the state, a little money for bread. The refugees are not required to pay taxes either. All Chingis Huseyn wants, however, is to return to his old home. "With God's help, we will make it back."

In the Agdjabedi region, many refugees are in the same situation as Huseynov, not having had the opportunity to move into new lodgings. A little outside of the new refugee settlement Lachin (here too, named after the old home), a dusty track runs past a residential estate under construction. Within sight of the construction site, however, many families are still living in subhuman conditions. Their makeshift shacks consist of copestones, clay and wood cobbled together, some with earth-covered roofs. The area is supplied with electricity, at least. Asgar Bagitov lives here too, with a family spanning three generations. He leads visitors into the main room of his dwelling, which is in fact underground. The walls are covered with pieces of cloth and the floor with rugs, the ceiling supported by a tree stump clad in plastic sheeting. The Bagitovs have been living here since 1992. "Our living conditions were far better in our homeland. We had water in front of our house, whereas here I have to walk up to four kilometres to get to a water hole," Asgar Bagitov tells me. He is thankful to the government for what little support they provide, but he hopes that the situation in which his sizeable family finds itself will improve soon. In six months, the Bagitovs are to receive a new house – only now, almost 20 years after they fled their home. "But we don't actually need a new house," says Asgar Bagitov, "we want our old land back instead." The area in which the refugees are stranded is very different to their old homeland, and not just due to the lack of accessible water. Instead of a fertile valley like Lachin, they now live on a barren, lowland plain.

It is a similar story for the two women we meet coming towards us on the unsealed road alongside. The women, Malahat Maeieva and Fatma Dunjamaljeva, live from subsistence farming supplemented with 15 Manat (around 12 euro) per month and they too are meant to receive a new house soon. What they actually want is to return to their former home, Vaqazin, a village about 50 kilometres north of the town of Lachin. They have bitter memories of their flight in 1992. Their father and brother were taken as hostages and could only follow them two years later. One fled, the other was released as part of an exchange. The women describe their own escape: right at the start, they were robbed of the sheep, clothes and shoes they had taken with them. On the way they survived by eating wild plants and after three weeks of walking, they reached Agdjabedi. As with many others, the longing for their occupied hometowns remains in the hearts of these women. Towns which for the most part now lie in ruins.

Severely affected regions along the line of control
According to Azerbaijan's state-issued statistics, there were a total of

**Stark belastete Regionen entlang
der Waffenstillstandslinien**

Gemäß Statistik des aserbaidschanischen Staates mit Stand vom
1. Oktober 2011 lebten von insgesamt 599 192 Vertriebenen zwar
über 185 000 in Baku und weitere 66 109 auf der benachbarten
Halbinsel Abseron. Aber die weit von der Hauptstadt entfernten
Distrikte mit ihren extremeren klimatischen Verhältnissen sind ver-
glichen mit ihrer Einwohnerzahl mit größeren Flüchtlingszahlen kon-
frontiert. Barda (33 582 Flüchtlinge, davon alleine 18 311 aus Agdam
bei 142 000 Einwohnern) und insbesondere der nicht besetzte Teil
von Fizuli (66 594 Flüchtlinge bei 111 000 Einwohnern) sind von
der Problematik am stärksten betroffen.

Der Regionalgouverneur Shahin Mammadov in Aghdjabedi ist um
seine Aufgabe nicht zu beneiden. Die Provinz hat total 120 000
Einwohner, davon alleine mehr als 15 000 Flüchtlinge aus den
besetzten Regionen Lachin, Agdam, Fizuli, Khojavend, Kelbajar und
Zengilan. Auch aserbaidschanische Kurden leben hier in insgesamt
vier Siedlungen (die Kurden siedelten einst in Lachin, wo von 1923
bis 1929 sogar das sogenannte „Rote Kurdistan" existierte. Das „Rote
Kurdistan" erhielt in jenen Jahren von der Sowjetunion gar den
Status eines autonomen Oblasts/Bezirks und die Amtssprache war
ein kurdischer Dialekt). Zeltcamps gibt es in der Region Aghdjabedi
mittlerweile keine mehr, so Mammadov. Doch seien in diesen früher
Tausende von Kindern geboren worden. Einst sei die Stadt Agh-
djabedi noch wie ein Dorf gewesen, so Mammadov, dann habe der
Staat in den Ausbau der Infrastruktur und Sozialausgaben investiert
und innerhalb von fünf Jahren 20 Schulen errichtet. Auch in seinem
Büro fehlt das Porträt des Präsidenten Illham Aliyev nicht. Wenn in
Aserbaidschan Fortschritt stattfindet, wird er in Verbindung gebracht
mit dem aktuellen Staatschef und dessen Vater und Amtsvorgänger
Heydar Aliyev. Unter Heydar Aliyev wurde Aserbaidschan nach dem
Bergkarabach-Krieg stabilisiert und der Ölvertrag mit westlichen
Firmen abgeschlossen, welcher die Hauptantriebskraft zum nach
wie vor anhaltenden wirtschaftlichen Aufschwung darstellt. Viele in

Aserbaidschan hat dieser erreicht, auch in den von der Hauptstadt
entfernten Regionen ist er spürbar. Aber trotzdem leben viele der
Flüchtlinge in Armut.

Auch in Kücerli im etwas nördlicher gelegenen Bezirk Terter
existieren nur rudimentäre Siedlungen. Nach dem Krieg lebten
Flüchtlinge gar in Güterwaggons. Jetzt säumen Lehmhütten die
Bahnlinie. Die Züge fahren von hier aus nicht weiter; Kücerli
ist die Endstation vor den besetzten Gebieten. In der Kleinstadt
Barda wurde öffentliche Infrastruktur wie Schulgebäude oder eine
Turnhalle zu Unterkünften umfunktioniert. In einer alten, kleinen
Sporthalle hausen beispielsweise neun Familien mit gegen 35 Per-
sonen in Holzverschlägen. Die Bewohner klagen über die misslichen
Umstände: Die Wasserleitung funktioniert nicht, die sanitären
Einrichtungen sind ungenügend, es hat Ratten. „Ich brauche Medikamente hier unter diesen Umständen", sagt ein Flüchtling und zeigt
einen Sack mit Arzneien. „Medikamente sind teuer. Wir leiden seit
20 Jahren, fordern Sie die Welt zur Aufmerksamkeit auf."

Apokalyptische Szenerie

In Hasankaya im Bezirk Terter könnte man meinen, der Krieg sei erst
vor Kurzem zu Ende gegangen, dabei sind 20 Jahre seit den Kämpfen
in dieser Region vergangen. Häuserskelette ragen aus der trostlosen
und kargen Landschaft empor. In behelfsmässigen Hütten haben sich
ein paar Familien mehr schlecht als recht eingerichtet, in unmittelbarer Nachbarschaft zu zerstörten Häusern. Vor einer Ruine ein
Autowrack, Rauch steigt empor. Eine Frau schaufelt einen kleinen
Graben, vermutlich für eine Wasserleitung, bei ihr drei Kinder. Ihr
Zuhause – die Ruine. Im Erdgeschoss des Gebäudes haben sie sich
eingerichtet, vom Obergeschoss fehlen viele Teile der Wände und
das Dach, so dass jene Etage unbewohnbar ist. Dann treffen wir in
der Nähe einen Mann mit seiner Tochter. Sie ist 24 Jahre alt; seit
sie vier ist, hört sie nichts mehr, weil während des Kriegs direkt
neben ihr eine Granate explodiert ist. Die junge Frau hat nie die
Gebärdensprache gelernt. Die Hauptstadt Baku, die Vorteile der

599,192 displaced persons as of 1 October 2011, of which more than 185,000 were living in Baku and a further 66,109 on the neighbouring Absheron peninsula. When compared to the size of resident populations, however, it is the districts far from the capital which were faced with the greatest refugee burden, areas already labouring under extreme climatic conditions. Barda took on 33,582 refugees (including 18,311 from Agdam alone) on top of its existing 142,000 residents, while the unoccupied part of Fizuli added 66,594 refugees to its previous population of 111,000. These areas were among the most heavily affected by the influx.

Agdjabedi regional governor Shahin Mammadov is not to be envied his task. The province has a total of 120,000 inhabitants, of which more than 15,000 are refugees from the occupied regions of Lachin, Agdam, Fizuli, Khojavend, Kalbajar and Zangilan. Azerbaijani Kurds live here too, in four settlements. The Kurds were previously settled in Lachin, where there even existed the so-named "Red Kurdistan" from 1923 to 1929. Mammadov says there are no more tent camps in the Agdjabedi region, though thousands of children were born in them while they existed. Before the arrival of the refugees, the city of Agdjabedi was still like a village, he says, and then the state invested heavily in building infrastructure and in social expenditure. Within five years, twenty new schools were opened. In Mammadov's office hangs the portrait of president Illham Aliyev. If progress is made in Azerbaijan, he will be associated with the current head of state and Heydar Aliyev, his father and predecessor in office. Under Heydar Aliyev's leadership, Azerbaijan was stabilised following the ravages of the Nagorno-Karabakh War and the oil contract with western companies was successfully negotiated, which was and still is the driving force behind the country's ongoing economic revival. This upturn in prosperity has benefited many in Azerbaijan, including those in regions far from the capital; there too, the economic recovery is noticeable. Yet despite this, many refugees still live in poverty. In the Tartar district a little to the north, in Kyucharli, again we find only rudimentary settlements. Following the war, refugees here lived in freight wagons. Now mud-walled huts hem the railway line. The trains go no further than this; Kyucharli is the last stop before the occupied territories. In the nearby township of Barda, public infrastructure such as school buildings and a gymnasium have been converted into accommodation. In one rather small old sports hall, for instance, nine families comprising around 35 people are housed in makeshift dwellings of wooden crating. The inhabitants complain of miserable conditions: the water supply is not working, the sanitary facilities are insufficient and there are rats. "Here, in these conditions, I need medicine," says one refugee, indicating a bag of tablets. "But medicine is expensive. We have been suffering for 20 years – please ask the world to take notice."

Apocalyptic Scenery
In Gasankaya, in the Tartar Rayon, one could be forgiven thinking that the war had only recently ended, though in fact twenty years have passed since this region last saw fighting. The skeletons of houses loom high over the bleak and barren landscape. A few families have knocked together improvised huts in close vicinity to the ruined houses. Smoke rises from a car wreck in front of one of the ruins while a woman digs a small ditch, presumably for a water pipe, with her three children at her side. The ruin is her home. They have settled as best they can in the ground floor of the building; the upper floor is missing many pieces of walls and the roof too, rendering it uninhabitable. Soon after, we come across a man walking with his daughter. She is twenty-four years old but has been deaf since she was four, when a shell exploded right next to her during the war. The young woman has never learnt sign language. The capital Baku and the advantages of civilisation – such as suitable care for the injured – are simply too far away.

The scenery here in Gasankaya, which lies only about a kilometre from the line of control, looks truly apocalyptic. The dry ground doesn't make life any easier. The previous inhabitants have abandoned the town and only one old man says that he used to live here

Zivilisation und somit eine adäquate Betreuung für die Versehrte sind zu weit entfernt.

Die Szenerien hier in Hasankaya, welches etwa einen Kilometer von der Waffenstillstandslinie entfernt liegt, sind wahrlich apokalyptisch. Der trockene Boden macht das Leben hier nicht viel besser. Die frühere Bevölkerung hat die Ortschaft verlassen. Nur ein alter Mann sagt, er habe schon früher hier gelebt. Die anderen wenigen Einwohner sind Flüchtlinge aus der Region Kelbajar. Im Frühling 1993 sind sie mühevoll über das schneebedeckte Murovgebirge vor der Besetzung ihrer Heimat geflohen. Die Vertriebenen haben hier Zuflucht gefunden und fristen seit Jahren eine karge Existenz. Vertriebene zwischen Ruinen. Vertriebene, die von fast der gesamten Welt vergessen wurden. Nur gerade ein großer Wassertank des IKRK (Internationales Komitee vom Roten Kreuz) zeugt davon, dass man sich ihrer erbarmt.

Danach machen wir einen kurzen Halt bei einer ehemaligen landwirtschaftlichen Forschungsanstalt. Zwei der drei Hauptgebäude wurden dem Erdboden gleichgemacht. Das dritte steht allein in der Landschaft. Der kleine eingezäunte Vorgarten ist ausgedörrt, braun. Keine Pflanze wächst. Das Gebäude selbst weist Spuren von Gewalt auf. Einschusslöcher, Brandspuren. In einer Hälfte des Erdgeschosses haben sich Flüchtlinge einquartiert. Von diesem Gebäude aus bietet sich ein imposanter Blick über die grüne, tiefer liegende Ebene des Flusses Terter hinweg zu den Bergen Bergkarabachs, den Ausläufern des Murovgebirges. Das Gebirge befindet sich im armenisch besetzten Teil des Distrikts Terter. Die Nachbardörfer Hasankayas liegen in Sichtweite. Auch sie sind Ruinenlandschaften.

in the past. The other residents, few as they are, are refugees from the Kalbajar region. In the spring of 1993, they made the laborious flight over the snow-covered mountain range Murovdag to escape the invasion of their homeland. The exiles found sanctuary here and have carved out a meagre existence for themselves in the years since. Exiles among ruins, exiles who have been forgotten by nearly the whole world. A large water tank belonging to the ICRC (the International Committee of the Red Cross) is the only evidence that their plight has aroused any compassion in the outside world.

Some time later, we make a brief stop at a former agricultural research institute. Two of the three main buildings have been razed to the ground. The third stands, all alone in its empty surrounds. The small front garden, neatly fenced in, is parched and brown; no plants are growing there now. The building itself bears evidence of violence, pitted with bullet holes and scorched by fire. In one half of the ground floor, refugees have taken up residence. Looking out from this building, however, we are rewarded with an impressive view of the green, low-lying flats of the river Tartar snaking away towards the mountains of Nagorno-Karabakh, the foothills of the Murovdag range. The range itself lies in the Armenian-occupied part of the Tartar district. Also within sight are the nearby villages, Gasankaya's neighbours. They, too, are ravaged landscapes, composed of ruins.

Chingis Huseyn Huseynov mit Familie,
zwischen Beylagan und Aghjabedi (März 2011)

Chingis Huseyn Huseynov and family
near Beylagan and Agdjabedi (March 2011)

Flüchtling, der beim Bahngeleise wohnt,
Kücerli, Rayon Terter (Oktober 2012)

Refugee living near the railway tracks,
Kyucharli, Tartar Rayon (October 2012)

Flüchtlingssiedlung bei Aghjabedi
(März 2011)

Refugee settlement near Agdjabedi
(March 2011)

Das Wohnzimmer der Familie Bagitov befindet sich unter der Erde,
Flüchtlingssiedlung bei Aghjabedi (März 2011)

The Bagitov family's living room is situated underground,
refugee settlement near Agdjabedi (March 2011)

Asgar Bagitov muss das Wasser vier Kilometer vom Haus entfernt holen,
Flüchtlingssiedlung bei Aghjabedi (März 2011)

Asgar Bagitov has to get the water four kilometers away from home,
refugee settlement near Agdjabedi (March 2011)

Asgar Bagitov mit seiner Frau,
Flüchtlingssiedlung bei Aghjabedi (März 2011)

Asgar Bagitov with his wife,
refugee settlement near Agdjabedi (March 2011)

Flüchtlinge aus Vagazin (Rayon Lachin),
Flüchtlingssiedlung bei Aghjabedi (März 2011)

Refugees from Vaqazin (Lachin Rayon),
refugee settlement near Agdjabedi (March 2011)

Flüchtlinge in Küche mit behelfsmäßigem Dach,
Barda (Oktober 2012)

Refugees in a kitchen with a makeshift roof,
Barda (October 2012)

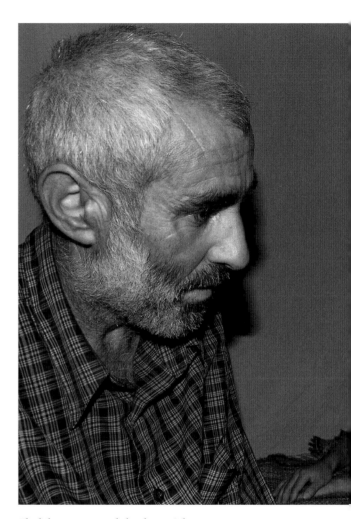

Flüchtling mit seiner behinderten Schwester,
Barda (Oktober 2012)

Refugee with his disabled sister,
Barda (October 2012)

Flüchtlinge, Barda (Oktober 2012)

Refugees, Barda (October 2012)

Flüchtlingskinder werden in sehr kleinen Baracken unterrichtet,
Rayon Barda (Oktober 2012)

Refugee children are taught in very small sheds,
Barda Rayon (October 2012)

Lehrer Elvin Duniyamaliyev unterrichtet die 6. Klasse, Rayon Barda (Oktober 2012)

Teacher Elvin Duniyamaliyev teaches the sixth form, Barda Rayon (Oktober 2012)

*Flüchtlingssiedlung entlang der stillgelegten Bahnlinie
Barda-Agdam, Endstation Kücerli,
Rayon Terter (Oktober 2012)*

*Refugee settlement along the abandoned railway line
Barda-Agdam, final station Kyucharli,
Tartar Rayon (October 2012)*

Die Flüchtlinge wohnten nach der Flucht zuerst in Bahnwaggons und bauten nachher behelfsmässige Unterkünfte entlang der Geleise, Kücerli, Rayon Terter (Oktober 2012)

After fleeing, the refugees lived first in railway wagons and later built improvised accommodation along the track, Kyucharli, Tartar Rayon (October 2012)

Flüchtlinge aus Kelbajar, wohnhaft in Hasankaya,
Rayon Terter (Oktober 2012)

Refugees originally from Kalbajar, now living in Gasankaya,
Tartar Rayon (October 2012)

Flüchtlinge von Kelbajar, wohnhaft in Hasankaya,
Rayon Terter (Oktober 2012)

Refugees from Kelbajar, now living in Hasankaya,
Terter Rayon (October 2012)

Hasankaya,
Rayon Terter (Oktober 2012)   *Gasankaya,*
Tartar Rayon (October 2012)

Wasserreservoir in Hasankaya,
Rayon Terter (Oktober 2012)

Water reservoir in Gasankaya,
Tartar Rayon (October 2012)

Vater mit seiner 24-jährigen gehörlosen Tochter. Sie hatte bisher keine Möglichkeit, die Gebärdensprache zu lernen, Hasankaya, Rayon Terter (Oktober 2012)

Father with his 24-year-old deaf daughter. She has never had the opportunity to learn sign language, Gasankaya, Tartar Rayon (October 2012)

*Ehemalige landwirtschaftliche Forschungsanstalt im Niemandsland bei Hasankaya
und Maragha. Eine Hälfte des Erdgeschosses wird von Flüchtlingen bewohnt,
Rayon Terter (Oktober 2012)*

*Former agricultural research institute in the no-man's-land
near Gasankaya and Maragha,
Tartar Rayon (October 2012)*

Flüchtlinge aus Kelbajar, wohnhaft in Hasankaya,
Rayon Terter (Oktober 2012)

Refugees originally from Kalbajar, now living in Gasankaya,
Tartar Rayon (October 2012)

121

06

SEHNSUCHT UND ERINNERUNGEN

Einsam hütet ein Hirte in der kargen Landschaft von Zobjug auf einer Anhöhe seine Schafe. Das Gebiet ist wüstenartig. Unwirtlich. Fernab von den fruchtbaren Tiefebenen Aserbaidschans, viele Fahrtstunden weg von der Hauptstadt Baku im Hinterland, nahe der Grenze zu Iran. Es ist später Nachmittag. Zobjug umfasst fünf Siedlungen und liegt in der Provinz Fizuli. Hier leben Flüchtlinge, die 1993 während des Krieges um Bergkarabach ihre Heimat, benachbarte aserbaidschanische Bezirke, aufgrund der Besetzung durch die armenischen Truppen verlassen mussten. Die Häuschen der Vertriebenen sind relativ modern, die Siedlungen erst vor wenigen Jahren erstellt worden. In den meisten kleinen Gärten wird etwas angepflanzt. Es existiert ein ansehnliches Schulgebäude. Wenige Kilometer von diesen künstlich in die Landschaft gestellten Dörfchen entfernt verläuft die ehemalige Front. Hinter dieser Linie liegen die von den Armeniern besetzten Provinzen Aserbaidschans inklusive Bergkarabach. Die Heimat der Flüchtlinge ist mit einer Distanz von nur ein paar Kilometern hier so nah und doch so fern, weil die Waffenstillstandslinie eine Rückkehr, ja sogar nur einen kurzen Besuch verunmöglicht. An diesem späten Nachmittag befinden sich Cechran Khudaverdi und einige andere Männer an einer Straße zu einem Siedlungsteil von Zobjug. Khudaverdi und seine Kollegen arbeiteten in der Sowjetzeit als Lehrer, Journalisten, Regierungsangestellte, in der Landwirtschaft auf Sowchosen oder Kolchosen. Nun müssen sie hier in Zobjug tatenlos ausharren. In dieser Gegend von Aserbaidschan gibt es

nicht viel zu tun. Es herrscht Arbeitslosigkeit. Immerhin erhalten die Flüchtlinge finanzielle Unterstützung durch den Staat. „Wir sind bereit, zurückzukehren. Wir möchten wieder die Gräber unserer Urahnen besuchen. Wenn sie das Friedensabkommen unterzeichnen, wären wir auch bereit, mit den Armeniern zusammenzuleben", sagt einer. Sie reden emotional, aber ohne erkennbaren Hass. Ein großer Schritt angesichts des erduldeten Leids.

„Tag und Nacht denken wir daran, zurückzukehren und die Gräber unserer Vorfahren in der Heimat zu besuchen", sagt auch Savanshiz Hasay Zeynalov in der Flüchtlingssiedlung Khojavend (benannt nach der alten Heimat) im Bezirk Aghdjabedi. Ursprünglich lebten er und seine Frau Genia in Salatekin, Rayon Khojavend. Heute teilen auch sie das Schicksal Vieler in Aserbaidschan, die aus ihrer früheren Heimat fliehen mussten. Der Bergkarabach-Krieg konfrontierte die junge Republik Aserbaidschan, deren ökonomische Verhältnisse und politische Strukturen in den Wirren nach dem Zusammenbruch der Sowjetunion noch nicht so gefestigt waren wie heute, mit Hunderttausenden Flüchtlingen. In Zeltcamps, ausrangierten Zugwaggons und Notunterkünften wurden die Entwurzelten lange Zeit untergebracht. In den letzten Jahren, in denen Aserbaidschan dank der Erdöl- und Gasvorkommen seine Staatseinnahmen enorm steigern konnte, wurden viele der neuen Flüchtlingsdörfer aus dem Boden gestampft.

Wie durchschnittlich das Ehepaar Zeynalov auf den ersten Blick auch scheinen mag, seine Geschichte ist bemerkenswert. Genia Zeynalovas Familienname vor der Hochzeit lautete Jessayan, sie ist ethnisch armenischer Herkunft und stammt aus dem Dorf Böyük Taglar am Fuße des Bergs Böyuk Kirs. Seit 53 Jahren verheiratet, haben die Zeynalovs heute vier Kinder sowie Groß- und Urgroßkinder, welche in Baku leben. Genia Zeynalova musste aufgrund ihrer ethnischen Herkunft in ihrem persönlichen Umfeld nie Angst haben, erzählt sie; ihr sei von den Verwandten ganz klar vermittelt worden, dass sie zu der Familie ihres Mannes gehöre. So war es auch klar, wem sie

06

YEARNING AND REMEMBERING

In the barren landscape of Zobjug, a solitary shepherd tends his sheep up on a hill. The surrounds are desert-like, inhospitable. We are a long way from the fertile flatlands of Azerbaijan and many hours' drive from the capital Baku, out in the backcountry near the Iranian border. It is late afternoon. Zobjug encompasses five settlements and is found in Fizuli Province. The residents are refugees, Azerbaijanis who had to abandon their homes during the 1993 Nagorno-Karabakh War when Armenian troops spilled over into their neighbouring districts and took possession of them as well. The little houses assigned to the refugees are relatively modern, as the settlement was built only a few years ago, with plants growing in most of the small gardens. There is even a respectable-looking schoolhouse. These hamlets, artificially installed in the landscape, lie just kilometres from the former front. Beyond this line are the Armenian-occupied provinces of Azerbaijan, including Nagorno-Karabakh. Here, at a distance of a few kilometres, the refugees' homeland is so near and yet so far, as the ceasefire line makes a return or even a short visit impossible. On this late afternoon, Cechran Khudaverdi and some other men stand by the side of a road in one of the settlements in Zobjug. During the Soviet period, Khudaverdi and his colleagues worked as teachers, journalists, government officials and in agriculture on sovkhozes and kolkhozes. Now they must hold out here in Zobjug, idle. In this part of Azerbaijan there is not a lot to do. The refugees receive financial support from the state but unemployment reigns supreme. "We are

ready to return. We would like to visit the graves of our ancestors once more. If they sign the peace treaty, we would also be prepared to live together with the Armenians," says one. They speak with emotion, but without discernable hate. This is a considerable stride, considering the hardships they have endured.

"Day and night we think about returning, about visiting the graves of our ancestors," says Savanshiz Hasay Zeynalov of the refugee settlement Khojavend (named after the old home town) in the Agdjabedi district. Originally, he and his wife Genia lived in Salaketin, in the Khojavend rayon. Now they share the fate of many other Azerbaijanis who were expelled from their previous homes. The Nagorno-Karabakh War confronted the Republic of Azerbaijan with hundreds of thousands of refugees, a considerable challenge for the young nation whose economic condition and political structures in the wake of the Soviet Union's collapse were far less stable than today. The displaced people were housed for a long time in tent camps, decommissioned railway carriages and emergency shelters. In recent years, Azerbaijan has increased its revenue dramatically thanks to its oil and gas deposits, and in this time many of the refugee villages have been built almost overnight.

However average the Zeynalovs might look at first sight, the married couple's story is noteworthy. Genia Zeynalova's maiden name was Jassaian; she is of ethnic Armenian origin and comes from the village Böyük Taglar at the foot of the Böyük Kirs Mountain. Married for 53 years, the Zeynalovs now have four children as well as grandchildren and great-grandchildren, who live in Baku. Genia Zeynalova has never had cause to feel afraid in her social environment because of her ethnic background, she tells me. When she was married, her relatives explained to her in no uncertain terms that she belonged now to her husband's family. Thus it was also clear whom she would follow. From the new family's side it was understood that, "You are one of us and can come with us." The now 74-year-old expresses her wish for a solution to the conflict; she would like to return home, to

folgen würde. „Du bist eine von uns und kannst mit uns kommen", hieß es. Die heute 74-Jährige sagt, dass sie sich eine Lösung des Konfliktes wünscht und zurück in die Heimat will, die aserbaidschanisches Territorium sei. Über die jetzige Lebenssituation wollen sich Zeynalovs aber nicht beschweren. „Wir können nicht unglücklich darüber sein, dass wir ein Haus in der Flüchtlingssiedlung bekommen haben." Doch auch das Ehepaar Zeynalov verspürt wie die anderen Flüchtlinge den Wunsch, zurückzukehren, dorthin, wo man einst vor dem Krieg lebte. „Es ist besser, in der Heimat zu leben und zu sterben", sagt Savanshiz Hasay Zeynalov. „Die Leute sind müde von der Situation. Die OSZE-Mitgliedsländer sollten sich endlich Gedanken machen über uns Menschen, die frei und normal leben möchten."

Ein weiterer Besuch im gleichen Flüchtlingsdorf gilt Sevil Azizova. Sie erzählt von den Zeiten vor dem Krieg im Distrikt Khojavend in Bergkarabach. Zu Sowjetzeiten habe mit Ausnahme eines Zwischenfalls in Stepanakert/Khankendi im Jahre 1968 Ruhe geherrscht. Armenier und Aserbaidschaner hätten gar untereinander geheiratet, man habe sich geholfen, auch wenn die einzelnen Dörfer meist monoethnisch bewohnt waren. „Wir hatten gute Lebensumstände, waren zufrieden." Ihr Mann führte ein Geschäft, sie arbeitete als Verkäuferin. Sie hatten damals ein Haus mit Umschwung, besassen Ziegen und Kühe, konnten sich mit Landwirtschaft selbst versorgen. „Unser Dorf lag perfekt, schöne Natur, Flüsse mit klarem Wasser. Wir waren glücklich – bis 1988." Dann begann der Druck der Armenier, die Repressionen gegen die aserbaidschanische Bevölkerungsminderheit in Bergkarabach wuchsen. Zunächst wurden die Aserbaidschaner aus höheren beruflichen Positionen gefeuert. Später folgten tätliche Angriffe. „Auf dem Weg in andere Dörfer wurde man mit Steinen beworfen oder gar beschossen. Während des Tages war es zwar einigermassen ruhig, aber von Sonnenuntergang bis zum Morgen hatten die Leute Angst, aus dem Haus zu gehen", erinnert sich Sevil Azizova. Dann folgten Schiessereien auch tagsüber, die Gewalttätigkeiten der Armenier gegen die aserbaidschanische

Zivilbevölkerungsminderheit in der Gegend eskalierten. Geiseln wurden genommen, „bei lebendigem Leib verbrannt, Mädchen die Finger abgeschnitten, um die Ringe zu nehmen, Goldzähne wurden entnommen. An einem Tag wurden 55 Menschen getötet. Es war nicht einmal möglich, die Leute zu beerdigen". Die Armenier hätten schließlich auch die Straßen gesperrt, so dass die einzige Fluchtmöglichkeit nach Agdam per Helikopter bestand. Der Wunsch Azizovas ist es, dass jeder in seine Heimat zurückkehren kann, dorthin, wo man aufgewachsen sei. Sie hofft, dass die Armenier diese besetzten Territorien eines Tages freigeben.

Die Flüchtlingssiedlung im Bezirk Aghdjabedi, in der Zeynalovs und Azimovs und weitere über 3000 Menschen leben, ist nach der alten Heimat Khojavend benannt. Die rechte Hand des Bürgermeisters, Shaiq Aslanov, zeigt an einer Wand im alten Verwaltungsgebäude des Dorfes auf eine Gedenktafel. Er kennt alle Geschichten der im Krieg Umgekommenen und Gefallenen. Bürgermeister Eyvaz Huseynov kommandierte die Bürgerwehr in Khojavend im Krieg. Huseynov erzählt, wie schon 1988, lange vor dem Ausbruch des eigentlichen Waffengangs die ersten Zivilisten getötet wurden. Wie schon 1988 den ethnischen Aserbaidschanern von Armeniern und Russen die Jagdwaffen abgenommen und 1991 drei Dörfer niedergebrannt wurden. Einzelne Dörfer im Rayon Khojavend und auch in anderen Teilen Bergkarabachs waren großmehrheitlich ethnisch aserbaidschanisch bevölkert und bildeten so quasi eine ethnische aserbaidschanische Enklave in der ethnisch mehrheitlich armenischen Enklave Bergkarabach. Daraus lässt sich auch die systematisch und offenbar von langer Hand geplante Vertreibung erklären, die mit der Einnahme der Ortschaften Tugh, Salatekin und Khojavend im Herbst 1991, dem Beschuss eines zivilen Busses am 18. September 1991 in Qaradagli und dem Massaker in der gleichen Ortschaft am 17. Februar 1992 ihre traurigen Höhepunkte erreichte. Im 800 Einwohner zählenden Qaradagli wurden damals 34 Menschen geköpft, 29 als Geiseln genommen und viele verwundet, so Huseynov. Ein paar Tage später folgte etwa zehn Kilometer nordöstlich das Massaker in Khojali,

what is after all Azerbaijani territory. That said, the Zeynalovs don't want to complain about their current living situation. "We can't be unhappy about having been given a house in the refugee settlement." Nonetheless, the Zeynalov couple, like the other refugees, still feels the pull to return to where they lived before the war. "It is better to live and die in one's homeland," says Savanshiz Hasay Zeynalov. "People are tired of the situation. The OSCE member countries should give some thought to us, at long last, people who just want to live a free and normal life."

I pay a second visit in the same refugee village, this time for an audience with Sevil Azizova. She talks about the times before the war in the district of Khojavend, Nagorno-Karabakh. In the Soviet times, with the exception of a 1968 incident in Stepanakert/Khankendi, peace prevailed. Armenians and Azerbaijanis intermarried and supported each other, even if individual villages were mostly inhabited by one ethnicity or the other. "We had good living conditions and we were content." Her husband ran a shop and she worked as a shop assistant. Back then they had a house with land around it, owned goats and cows, and with their farming they were self-sufficient. "Our village was perfectly situated, with beautiful nature and clear flowing rivers. We were happy – until 1988." Then the Armenians began to apply pressure, and repression of the minority Azeri population in Nagorno-Karabakh grew. At first, Azerbaijanis were fired from higher professional positions. Later came physical assaults. "Going down the road to other villages, we would have stones thrown at us or even be shot at. During the day it was fairly quiet but from sundown until the following morning, people were afraid to leave their houses," recalls Sevil Azizova. Next, the incidents of gunfire spread into the daylight hours as well and the violent attacks of the Armenians against the minority civilian Azerbaijani population in the area increased in severity. Hostages were taken, "burnt alive, girls' fingers were cut off to take their rings, gold teeth were pulled out and stolen. In one day, 55 people were killed. It wasn't even possible to bury the dead." In the end, she says, the Armenians shut off the roads so that the

only escape route to Agdam was by helicopter. Azizova's wish is that everyone may return to their homelands, to the places where they grew up. She still has hope that the Armenians will one day release the occupied territories.

The refugee settlement in the Agdjabedi district in which the Zeynalovs, the Azimovs and more than 3,000 other people live, has been named after their old home, Khojavend. Shaiq Aslanov, the mayor's right-hand man, points at a memorial plaque on the wall of the town's old administrative building. He knows the stories of all those who perished and fell in the war. Town mayor Eyvaz Huseynov commanded Khojavend's civil defence during the war. He recounts how the first civilians were killed as early as 1988, long before the outbreak of war proper. That already in 1988, the Armenians and Russians confiscated the ethnic Azerbaijanis' hunting weapons, how in 1991 three villages were burnt to the ground. Several towns in the Khojavend rayon and in other parts of Nagorno-Karabakh had overwhelmingly ethnic Azeri populations and constituted as such almost an ethnic Azerbaijani enclave within the predominantly Armenian enclave Nagorno-Karabakh. This goes to explain the systematic expulsion of these inhabitants – clearly planned well in advance – which culminated in the taking of the villages Tugh, Salaketin and Khojavend in autumn 1991, the shelling of a civilian bus in Qaradagli on 18 September 1991, and the massacre on 17 February 1992, in the same town. In Qaradagli, a town of 800 inhabitants, 34 people were beheaded, 29 taken hostage and many more wounded, according to Huseynov. Some days later and just 10 kilometres to the northeast followed the massacre of Khojaly, where 613 Azerbaijanis were killed, including many women and children.

Eyvaz Huseynov tells us that the early times were very difficult for the people living in exile. The buildings and camps had no heating. Schools and hospitals were lacking. When the then Azerbaijani president Heydar Aliyev signed the much-heralded "Contract of the Century" for the exploitation of Azerbaijan's huge oil and gas reserves

bei dem 613 Aserbaidschaner, darunter viele Frauen und Kinder, den Tod fanden. Eyvaz Huseynov erzählt, die erste Zeit für die Flüchtlinge im Exil sei hart gewesen. In den Gebäuden und Camps gab es keine Heizung. Auch Schulen und Spitäler fehlten damals. Als der damalige aserbaidschanische Präsident Heydar Aliyev den als „Contract of the Century" gepriesenen Vertrag für die Förderung riesiger Öl- und Gasvorkommen mit westlichen Rohstoffunternehmen unterzeichnet hatte, sei das Schicksal der Flüchtlinge als Hauptproblem des Landes deklariert worden und Geld in die Versorgung dieser Kriegsopfer geflossen. „Als Flüchtling habe ich auch gelitten, alle Verwandten mussten fliehen – zum Teil verwundet." Huseynov hat als junger Mann in Baku studiert, aber nachher in der Heimat keine adäquate Arbeit bekommen. „Die Regierung (in Bergkarabach, Anm. des Autors) war ja schließlich armenisch", sagt er. Zur Zeit des Krieges sei Aserbaidschan kein Staat wie jetzt gewesen. Er sinniert: „Jetzt sind wir stark. Wir kennen die Armenier. Ich denke nicht, dass es eine friedliche Lösung gibt. Sie spielen auf Zeit, denken wohl, wir vergessen und vergeben." Dennoch sagt aber auch er, „wir lebten damals mit ihnen und würden auch wieder mit ihnen leben". Das sei auch das Ansinnen der aserbaidschanischen Gemeinschaft Bergkarabachs, einer Vereinigung der Flüchtlinge.

Nach dem Gespräch gehe ich hinaus vor das Verwaltungsgebäude. Es ist ein späterer Nachmittag. Die Sonne steht etwas tiefer. Viele junge Knaben tummeln sich auf dem zentral gelegenen Dorfplatz, die Schule ist aus. Die Kinder spielen. Als sie den Fotoapparat entdecken, eilen viele herbei, um aufs Bild zu gelangen. Diese Jungs, die nun in die Linse lachen, haben die Heimat ihrer Eltern nie mit ihren eigenen Augen gesehen. Sie kennen das Land ihrer Vorfahren nur aus Erzählungen. Es ist die erste Generation Aserbaidschaner, die im Exil aufwächst. Ob sie später als Erwachsene noch den Wunsch verspüren werden, in der Heimat der Eltern zu leben?

with western natural resources companies, the fate of the refugees was declared the country's most pressing concern and funds began to flow towards providing for these victims of war. "As a refugee, I too have suffered. All my relatives had to flee, some of them injured." As a younger man, Huseynov studied in Baku, but subsequently could find no suitable work in his homeland. "The Government [in Nagorno-Karabakh] was Armenian, after all," he says. At the time of the war, Azerbaijan was not at all the country it has now become. He ponders the future. "Now we are strong and we know the Armenians. I don't think that there is a peaceful answer. They are playing for time, and probably think we will forgive and forget." But then he adds, "We lived with them then and we would live with them again." The Azerbaijani Community of Nagorno-Karabakh, a refugee association, shares this attitude.

Following this discussion, I leave the administrative building and stand outside. It is late afternoon and the sun is sitting low in the sky. School is out and a group of young boys are romping around the central village square. The children are playing, but once they spot the camera they rush over to get into the picture. These boys who now laugh into the lens have never seen their parents' homeland with their own eyes. They know the country of their forebears only from stories. This is the first generation of Azerbaijanis who are growing up in exile. Will they later, as adults, still feel the desire to live in the land of their parents?

Neue Flüchtlingssiedlung Zobjug im Südwesten
Aserbaidschans nahe der iranischen Grenze,
Rayon Fizuli (2009)

New refugee settlement Zobjug in the south-west of
Azerbaijan near the Iranian border,
Fizuli Rayon (2009)

Flüchtlinge aus Fizuli,
Zobjug, Rayon Fizuli (August 2009)

Refugees from Fizuli,
Zobjug, Fizuli Rayon (August 2009)

Ethnisch-gemischtes Ehepaar: Savanshiz Hasay Zeynalov mit Frau Genia (geborene Jessayan), Flüchtlingssiedlung Khojavend, Rayon Beylagan (August 2011)

Ethnically mixed married couple: Savanshiz Hasay Zeynalov with his wife Genia (maiden name Jessayan), refugee settlement Khojavend, Beylagan Rayon (August 2011)

Die Großfamilie von Sevila Azizova (vierte von links),
Flüchtlingssiedlung Khojavend,
Rayon Beylagan (März 2011)

Sevil Azizova (fourth from the left) with her extended
family, refugee settlement Khojavend,
Beylagan Rayon (March 2011)

Schulkinder im Zentrum der Flüchtlingssiedlung Khojavend,
Rayon Beylagan (März 2011)

Schoolchildren at the centre of the refugee settlement Khojavend,
Beylagan Rayon (March 2011)

Shaiq Aslanov, Assistent der Regionalbehörde,
vor der Ehrenwand Khojavends,
Flüchtlingssiedlung Khojavend, Rayon Beylagan (März 2011)

Shaiq Aslanov, local govenment assistant, in front of an honour
board for the fallen heroes of Khojavend,
refugee settlement Khojavend, Beylagan Rayon (March 2011)

Im Bau befindliche Flüchtlingssiedlung,
Rayon Aghjabedi (März 2011)

New refugee settlement under construction,
Agdjabedi Rayon (March 2011)

Neue Flüchtlingssiedlung Guzanli,
Rayon Agdam (Oktober 2012)

New refugee settlement Quzanli,
Agdam Rayon (October 2012)

07

DAS UNHEIL IM BODEN

„Wir unterscheiden zwischen Minenfeldern und Kampfgebiet", erzählt Habil Babayev. Er ist Gruppenführer bei der staatlichen aserbaidschanischen Minenräumungsgesellschaft ANAMA. Seine Männer sind draußen bei der Arbeit. Sie sollen Felder nach Minen und Blindgängern absuchen und davon räumen, damit das Gebiet für die Landwirtschaft genutzt werden kann. In ehemaligen Kampfgebieten finden sich sogenannte UXO (unexploded ordnance). Das können meist kleinere oder mittelgroße, teilweise oder gar nicht explodierte Geschosse sein, beispielsweise Handgranaten, aber auch Artilleriegeschosse. In Minenfeldern ist es nicht unüblich, dass auch Antipanzerminen entdeckt werden.

Die heutige Schicht hat früh begonnen, da im Landesinnern Aserbaidschans im Sommer tagsüber wegen der hohen Temperaturen an Arbeiten mit Schutzweste und Helm kaum zu denken ist. In einem Bereich suchen die Männer mit Metalldetektoren, im zweiten Feld pflügt ein ferngesteuerter, einem Mähdreschervorsatz ähnlicher Metallkoloss sich 20 Zentimeter in den Boden. Der Maschinenführer ist etwa 150 Meter vom Gefährt entfernt, um bei einer Detonation nicht getroffen zu werden. Eine Handvoll solcher Minenräumungsgeräte der slowenischen Marke Bozena stehen in Diensten der ANAMA-Basis Horadiz. Habil Babayev erklärt mittels einer Karte, wie das Arbeitsfeld unterteilt ist; im Hintergrund steht ein Ambulanzwagen mit Personal bereit. Für alle Fälle, sollte etwas schiefgehen. „Wie lautet Ihre Blutgruppe?", wird der Besucher sicherheitshalber gefragt.

Zwei Jahre Arbeit, eine Zone, 4,5 Kilometer lang und 320 Meter breit. Werden Minen oder Blindgänger gefunden, werden sie, wenn möglich, vor Ort zur Explosion gebracht. Ansonsten sammelt man sie ein und sprengt sie kontrolliert in die Luft. Die Minenräumer haben gesicherten Pfaden zu folgen. ANAMA stellt bei seinen Projekten vor Ort Männer aus den betroffenen Regionen als Minenräumer ein. Natürlich werden sie erst im Feld eingesetzt, wenn sie eine spezifische Ausbildung gemacht haben. Teamleader Habil Babayev arbeitet bereits seit acht Jahren bei ANAMA. Das hier zu räumende Feld sei, erzählt er, von Mitte 1993 bis 1994 wie andere Teile Fizulis von den Armeniern besetzt gewesen, ein Kampfgebiet an der Front. Deshalb finden sich hier viele Minen und Blindgänger. Zwei Antipanzerminen wurden in diesem Feld bereits entdeckt. Die Nachkontrollen führt man mit Suchhunden durch. Nach jeden paar Quadratmetern, die die Hunde abgeschnuppert haben, erhalten sie Komplimente ihrer Führer. „Für die Hunde ist das alles ein Spiel, deshalb müssen sie gelobt werden. Sonst verlieren sie schnell mal das Interesse daran", erklärt Ramasan Heydarov, der Hundebetreuer.

Immense Aufgabe
Die Organisation ANAMA wurde 1998 gegründet, um die gesamte Minen- und Blindgängerräumung in Aserbaidschan nach dem Bergkarabach-Krieg zu koordinieren. ANAMA beschäftigt heute insgesamt über 500 Leute. Die Aufgabe ist immens und wird noch viele Jahre lang dauern. In den Jahren 2001 bis 2003 wurden 480 Siedlungen als minenverseucht klassifiziert, weitere 163 von Blindgängern versehrt. Von 305 Quadratkilometern Aserbaidschans, die kontaminiert sind oder waren, sind große Teile noch nicht geräumt. Werden Bergkarabach und die anderen Provinzen befreit, rechnet man mit weiteren 350 bis 800 Quadratkilometern, die geräumt werden müssen. Derzeit unter armenischer Besatzung, findet dort die Minenräumung lediglich durch die HALO Trust (Sitz in Großbritannien) statt. Weil diese weniger Geld als in den Jahren zuvor von der britischen Regierung erhält, musste 2011 in Bergkarabach lokales Personal entlassen und die Aktivitäten reduziert werden.

07

AZERBAIJAN

EVIL IN THE GROUND

"We differentiate between minefields and combat zones," explains Habil Babayev. He is a group leader at the government-run Azerbaijani demining organisation ANAMA (Azerbaijan National Agency for Mine Actions). His men are outside, hard at work. They search fields for mines and unexploded shells and then clear them so that the land can be used for agriculture. In former combat zones, there is what is known as UXO (unexploded ordnance). This describes explosives which are only partly exploded or not at all. These are mostly small or medium-sized: hand grenades are one example, artillery shells another. In minefields it is not unusual to discover anti-tank mines as well.

Today's shift began early this morning, as the high temperatures experienced in Azerbaijan's interior in summer make working with protective vests and helmets in the middle of the day almost unthinkable. In one area, men are scouring the ground with metal detectors, while in another field a remote-controlled metal colossus resembling a combine harvester ploughs the earth at a depth of 20 centimetres. The machine's operator maintains a distance of about 150 metres from the vehicle itself, so as not to be hit in the event of a detonation. These demining machines are of the Slovenian make "Bozena" and the ANAMA base in Horadiz has a handful of them at its disposal. Habil Babayev explains with the aid of a map how the working area is divided up; at the very rear, an ambulance waits ready with staff on hand, just in case something should go wrong.

They are prepared for every contingency. "What is your blood type?" visitors are asked, as a precaution.

Two years' work: a stretch of land 4.5 kilometres long and 320 metres wide. When mines or live shells are found, they are detonated where they lie if possible; otherwise, they are collected and exploded under controlled conditions. The workers carrying out the demining follow paths that have already been certified as safe; these are local men, employed by ANAMA in the affected regions to work as deminers for its on-site projects. Before they step out into the field, of course, they must first complete a specialised training program. Team leader Habil Babayev has been working for ANAMA for eight years already. The field which is to be cleared here, he tells us, was occupied by the Armenians from mid-1993 until 1994, as were other parts of Fizuli. It was in fact a combat zone, which is why they are finding a large number of mines and unexploded shells here. Two anti-tank mines have been discovered in this particular field already. The final check is carried out with the help of search dogs, who are praised by their handler after every few square metres they sniff through. "For the dogs, it is all just a game, so they must be praised and encouraged as they go along. Otherwise they lose interest quickly," explains Ramasan Heydarov, who is in charge of the dogs.

A Mammoth Task

The organisation ANAMA was founded in 1998, in order to coordinate the nationwide clearing of mines and unexploded shells left over from the Nagorno-Karabakh War. ANAMA currently employs more than 500 people, but its task is immense and will require many more years of painstaking effort. In the period from 2001 to 2003, 480 settlements were classified as mine-contaminated, with a further 163 hampered by unexploded ordnance. Of the 305 square kilometres in Azerbaijan that were or are contaminated, vast tracts have not yet been cleared. If Nagorno-Karabakh and the other provinces were liberated, the demining project would be confronted with yet a further 350 to 800 square kilometres of land to be made safe. Since

Wegen der jahrelangen Erfahrung der Aserbaidschaner von ANAMA mit der Arbeit im Feld lassen sich mittlerweile Georgier, Afghanen, Tadschicken und Libanesen von ihnen in der Technik der Minenräumung unterweisen. In den Dörfern und Schulen wird die Bevölkerung über die Gefahr von Blindgängern informiert. Und bei Ganja im Nordwesten Aserbaidschans unterstützt ANAMA eine kleine Teppich- und Stoffwerkstatt, wo Familienangehörige von Minenopfern etwas Geld verdienen können.

Die Nacht ist mittlerweile über die Provinz Fizuli hereingebrochen. In einem Gebäude der ANAMA in Horadiz sitzt Hundeführer Ramasan Heydarov an einem Plastiktisch und trinkt Tee. Heydarov hat in der damaligen UdSSR Kynologie (Wissenschaft vom Hund) studiert und betreut zusammen mit einem Veterinär und einem weiteren Angestellten die 32 Minensuchhunde auf der Basis. Zuvor führte er Drogenspürhunde auf dem Flughafen von Baku. Und in den 80ern diente er der Roten Armee in Afghanistan. „In einem Spezialkommando" – weiter will er offenbar nicht darauf eingehen. „Ich habe keinen Computer und keinen Fernseher. Ich will von all der Gewalt in der Welt gar nichts mehr sehen. Wenn ich denke, was sich die Menschen so alles antun, bin ich zufrieden, hier mit den Hunden zu leben", sagt er.

Ehemalige Munitionsdepots

Neben der Minenräumung in an die Waffenstillstandslinie angrenzenden Regionen arbeitet ANAMA auch auf Arealen ehemaliger Munitionsdepots. Das größte Räumungsprojekt diesbezüglich dauerte fast vier Jahre: In Saloglu, einer Ortschaft im Bezirk Agstafa im Dreiländereck Aserbaidschan/Armenien/Georgien, befand sich zu Sowjetzeiten das größte Depot im südlichen Kaukasus. Als die Rote Armee im Zuge des Zerfalls der UdSSR und bei Ausbruch des Bergkarabach-Krieges ihren Rückzug antrat, sprengte sie die Basis in die Luft. Nach den Detonationen war in Saloglu und Umgebung schließlich auf einer Fläche von 5,6 Quadratkilometern das Gelände übersät mit Projektilen unterschiedlicher Größe, von Handgranaten über Geschosse bis zu Raketen. Einige Bunker waren noch gefüllt mit rostiger Munition. Und nicht nur über der Erde, auch unter der Oberfläche befanden sich die Blindgänger. Im Laufe der Jahre starben in und um Saloglu aufgrund dieser Überreste mehr als 30 Menschen, mehr als doppelt so viele wurden verletzt. In dieser Gegend mit Arbeitslosigkeit und ohne große Perspektiven forderte so auch das Einsammeln von Metall seinen Tribut.

Saloglus geografische Lage im Dreiländereck wirkte sich Anfang des neuen Jahrzehnts aus. Die Gegend wurde zum Transitkorridor. 2004 begannen die Arbeiten zum Bau der Ölpipeline Baku-Tiflis-Ceyhan. Das brachte die staatliche Minenräumungsgesellschaft ANAMA in die Region Agstafa. Ihr oblag es, auf einer Länge von 32 Kilometern einen rund 50 Meter breiten Streifen bis in eine Tiefe von drei Metern von Blindgängern zu säubern. Die Rohre sollten einen Meter unter den Boden, um die Gefahr von Anschlägen eindämmen zu können. An einer Stelle verlief die vorgesehene Pipelineroute nur wenige Meter vom Gelände der vormaligen sowjetischen Munitionsbasis entfernt. Rund 120 Projektile wurden im geplanten Pipelinebereich ausgehoben. ANAMA verblieb schließlich in der Region. Im Dezember 2005 begann die Organisation unter der Aufsicht von UNO und NATO mit der Blindgängerräumung des Areals in und um die Basis. Längst handelte es sich beim sowjetischen Erbe nicht nur um eine humanitäre Katastrophe, denn auch ökologische Gefahren drohten. Die alte Munition fing an zu rosten. Einige Blindgänger enthielten weißen Phosphor. Ein perfides Material, das hochgiftig ist und eine tödliche Wirkung entfalten kann. Das Ausmaß der Dekontaminierung war riesig, bis zum Ende wurden fast 600 000 Blindgänger weggeräumt. 250 verschiedene Munitionsarten sind es total, die identifiziert wurden. ANAMA hatte sogar eine Basis errichtet und beschäftigte in Saloglu alleine um die 70 Mitarbeiter. 2011 konnte das Gelände schließlich zur friedlichen Nutzung freigegeben werden.

Zwar sind bislang keine eindeutigen Eingeständnisse Moskaus bezüglich der Basis in Saloglu oder entsprechende Dokumente, die

it is currently under Armenian control, the only demining efforts taking place there are those carried out by the HALO Trust, based in Great Britain. This organisation has, however, received reduced funding from the British government in recent years and in 2011 was obliged to lay off local staff in Nagorno-Karabakh and to cut back its operations.

Since the Azerbaijanis of ANAMA have so many years of experience working in the field, their expertise is now being passed on to Georgians, Afghanis, Tajiks and Lebanese, who need to be instructed in their techniques of mine clearing. The educational component is important too; in villages and schools, local populations are informed about the dangers of unexploded ordnance. In Ganja, meanwhile, a city in northwest Azerbaijan, ANAMA supports a modest carpet and fabric workshop, where relatives of landmine victims are able to earn a little money.

By now, night has descended upon Fizuli province. In one of ANAMA's buildings in Horadiz, dog handler Ramasan Heydarov sits on a plastic table and slowly drinks his tea. Heydarov studied cynology (a specialist study of canines or domestic dogs) in the USSR and now is jointly responsible for the 32 mine search dogs at the base, together with a veterinarian and one other employee. Previously, he handled drug-sniffing dogs at Baku airport. Back in the 1980s he served in the Red Army in Afghanistan "in a special detachment," though he clearly does not want to go into any more detail. "I have neither a computer nor a television. I don't want to see anything more of all the violence in the world. When I think of all the things people do to each other, I'm happy to be living here with the dogs," he says.

Former ammunition depots

In addition to mine clearing in the regions bordering the ceasefire line, ANAMA also works on sites formerly used as ammunition depots. The largest depot clearance project lasted almost four years. This was in Saloglu, a village in the Agstafa district in the tri-border region of Azerbaijan, Armenia and Georgia, where during the Soviet era the largest arms depot in the southern Caucasus was located. Following the collapse of the USSR and the outbreak of the Nagorno-Karabakh War, the Red Army beat a retreat and blasted the base sky-high. After the detonation, Saloglu and its surrounds – altogether an area of 5.6 square kilometres – were littered with projectiles of all sizes, from hand grenades to artillery shells to rockets. A number of bunkers were still filled with rusty ammunition. The unexploded rounds lay not only on top of the ground but under the surface also. Over the course of years, more than 30 people died in and around Saloglu due to these remnants, with more than double that number injured. In this part of the country, with high unemployment and no great prospects in view, the risky business of metal collecting has exacted a high price.

Saloglu's geographic position in the border triangle became a deciding factor at the beginning of the new decade. The area first became a transit corridor and then in 2004, construction work on the Baku-Tbilisi-Ceyhan oil pipeline began. This brought the state-run mine-clearing body ANAMA into the Agstafa region. Their task was to clear a 32-kilometre-long, 50-metre-wide strip of land of all unexploded ordnance, to a depth of 3 metres. The pipeline was to be laid one metre beneath the ground as a protective measure, limiting the potential danger of attacks. At one point, the planned route of the pipeline ran at a distance of just a few metres from the grounds of the former Soviet ammunition base. About 120 projectiles were dug out of the area dedicated to the new pipeline. ANAMA ended up staying in the region and in December 2005 the organisation began work on decontaminating the area in and around the base, under the super-vision of the UN and NATO. By this time, the legacy of the Soviets had become not only a humanitarian catastrophe but also a dangerous ecological threat. The old munitions were starting to rust. Some of the unexploded shells contained white phosphorous, a particularly unpleasant substance which is highly poisonous and whose effects can be fatal. The scale of the decontamination project was enormous;

einen direkten Zusammenhang mit dem Bergkarabach-Konflikt zeigen, öffentlich geworden. Es gibt aber plausible Mutmaßungen, dass zu jener Zeit in der Region mit Munition gehandelt wurde. Thomas de Waal, Autor des Buches „Black Garden", das bezüglich des Bergkarabach-Konflikts als Standardwerk gilt, vermutet, dass die Russen von Munitionsbasen aus Verkäufe getätigt haben und „dann die Plätze in die Luft gesprengt haben, um Beweise dafür zu verdecken". Nazim Ismailov, Direktor von ANAMA, geht sogar noch weiter. In einem Dokument, von Wikileaks im Rahmen der „Cablegate"-Veröffentlichungen publik gemacht, ist festgehalten, dass Ismailov gegenüber dem russischen Vertreter auf einer Sitzung des Forums für Sicherheit der OSZE im Jahre 2008 den Vorwurf erhob, die Munition in Saloglu sei von den Sowjets bewusst zerstört worden, um sie vor dem Zugriff der Aserbaidschaner zu schützen. Die Vermutung ist gar nicht so verwegen: Die zeitliche und geografische Nähe zum Bergkarabach-Konflikt ist unwiderlegbar. Die Bemühungen der Konfliktparteien, an alte Munitionsbestände der Sowjets zu kommen, zeigen sich auch darin, dass 1992 laut der Los Angeles Times zehn russische Offiziere von Armeniern gekidnappt wurden, um Munitionsbestände zu erpressen.

in total, almost 600,000 unexploded devices were removed, with 250 different types of munitions identified. ANAMA even set up its own base and employed 70 workers in Saloglu alone. In 2011, the area was finally given clearance to be used for peaceful purposes.

To this day, Moscow has made no clear admissions regarding the base in Saloglu, nor have any relevant documents establishing a direct link with the Nagorno-Karabakh conflict been made public. There is nonetheless plausible conjecture that arms trading was taking place in the region at the time. Thomas de Waal, author of "Black Garden", the book regarded as the standard reference on the Nagorno-Karabakh conflict, suspects that the Russians at the weapons base did business in the sale of arms and "then blew the place up to hide the proof". Nazim Ismailov, the director of ANAMA, goes even further. In one document made public by Wikileaks as part of the "Cablegate" mass publications, there is a record of Ismailov reproaching Russia's representative at the 2008 sitting of the OSCE Forum for Security. He accuses the Soviets of having deliberately destroyed the arms depot in Saloglu in order to stop the Azerbaijanis from seizing it. The presumption is not altogether an audacious one; the chronological and geographic proximity to the Nagorno-Karabakh conflict is irrefutable. That the quarrelling parties went to great efforts to gain access to Soviet arms stocks is also known, as is illustrated by the 1992 incident reported by the Los Angeles Times, according to which ten Russian officers were kidnapped by Armenians in order to extort weapons holdings from them.

Minenräumer der staatlichen Organisation ANAMA,
Rayon Fizuli (August 2009)

Mine-clearing workers from the National Agency of Mine Action ANAMA,
Fizuli Rayon (August 2009)

Blindgängerräumung auf dem Gelände einer
ehemaligen sowjetischen Munitionsbasis,
Saloglu, Rayon Agstafa (March 2010)

Clearance of unexploded ordnance on the
site of a former Soviet ammunition base,
Saloglu, Agstafa Rayon (March 2010)

Hundeführer und Spürhund,
Rayon Terter (Oktober 2011)

Dog handler and sniffer dogs,
Tartar Rayon (October 2012)

Blindgängerverseuchtes Gelände in Saloglu,   *UXO-contaminated area in Saloglu,*
Rayon Agstafa (März 2010)   *Agstafa Rayon (March 2010)*

Aufgefundene Projektile und Minen,
Rayon Fizuli (August 2009)

Excavated projectiles and mines,
Fizuli Rayon (August 2009)

08

ASERBAIDSCHAN

WAFFEN UND
ZORNIGE HERZEN

Es ist eine schrittweise Annäherung an einen Ort der Fragilität. Mit einem Geländefahrzeug der Armee geht es in Richtung der „Kontaktlinie" im Rayon Fizuli. „Kontaktlinie" wird die Waffenstillstandslinie auch genannt, die die Stellungen der aserbaidschanischen Armee und die der armenischen Separatisten voneinander trennt. Am 12. Mai 1994 wurde zwischen Armenien und Aserbaidschan ein Waffenstillstandsabkommen unterzeichnet. Vorher gelang es der aserbaidschanischen Armee in der Gegend von Fizuli immerhin, die Separatisten etwas zurückzudrängen. Das erklärt auch, warum während der Fahrt Häuserruinen zu sehen sind. Hier tobte einst der Kampf. Oberstleutnant Sarvar Jebrailov berichtet, dass es an der Frontlinie immer wieder zu Schusswechseln komme. Die armenischen Scharfschützen seien meist zwischen 24 Uhr und 5 Uhr in der Früh aktiv. „Es sind spontane Schießereien ohne genaues Ziel. Eine typisch sowjetische Taktik, um die Moral der Soldaten hochzuhalten", meint er, „Provokationen." Auf dem Weg zum vordersten Schützengraben machen wir Halt bei einer Panzerstellung. Diese befindet sich einige Kilometer von der heißen Zone entfernt. Die T-72 stehen gut getarnt, leicht versenkt im Gelände. Junge Soldaten beüben das Gerät. Mit der Testfahrt eines Kampfpanzers will man uns dessen Gelenkigkeit zeigen. „Das sind die besten Panzer", bemerkt ein Verantwortlicher. Eine weitere Linie des aserbaidschanischen Dispositivs besteht aus Artillerie. Auch Überwachungsposten sind in dieser Gegend installiert.Es scheint, als hätte sich die Armee hier für die Ewigkeit

eingerichtet. Am Ende des Schützengrabens steht eine kleine Truppenunterkunft, ein stabiler Betonbau mit einem spärlich eingerichteten Bettenzimmer. Hier trennen die Soldaten nur etwa 200 Meter von den Linien der gegnerischen Separatisten. Dazwischen die Waffenstillstandslinie. Bestimmten Schrittes gehen die jungen Soldaten durch den etwa zwei Meter tiefen Graben. Durch einen kleinen Schlitz in einem Schützenstand sieht man das besetzte Land gegenüber. Ganz nahe an der Frontlinie und unmittelbar neben einer armenischen Stellung stehen Häuserruinen. In diesen Gebäuden lebt schon lange niemand mehr. Die einst in diesen nun zerstörten und verlassenen Dörfern ansässigen Aserbaidschaner hausen jetzt in den Flüchtlingssiedlungen.

Als Kind geflüchtet und nun in der Armee

„Wir können nicht vergessen, was sie uns angetan haben. Wie könnten wir je wieder mit Leuten zusammenleben, die unsere Verwandten getötet haben? Ich will das nicht", sagt Samir Aliyev. Der 23-Jährige gehört zum kleinen Trupp, der in diesem vordersten Schützengraben, einer entlegenen Stellung an der Front, Dienst tut, jeweils zwei Wochen am Stück. Samir Aliyev unterscheidet sich von seinen Kameraden: Er ist ein Flüchtling aus den jetzt armenisch besetzten Gebieten. Mit fünf Jahren musste Aliyev mit seiner Familie aus Lachin flüchten. Lachin, diese hügelige Region mit grünen Talböden und klarem Wasser in den Bächen und Flüsschen. Dort ist es ganz anders als in den trockenen, wüstenartigen Landstrichen Aserbaidschans, wo jetzt die Flüchtlinge in stereotypen Siedlungen oder ärmlichen Dörfern ihr Dasein fristen. In der Nacht vom 16. auf den 17. Mai 1992 fiel die Region in die Hände der Armenier. „Ich erinnere mich nicht mehr an die Flucht, aber an unser Haus neben der Moschee und an die Natur. Ich erinnere mich an die Kinder, an die Menschen." In Aliyevs Familie redet man noch oft über das frühere Leben in der verlorenen Heimat. „Wenn man seine Gefühle in sich drinnen lässt, explodieren sie sonst irgendwann einmal", sagt der junge Aserbaidschaner. Immer wieder kommen an der etwa 120 Kilometer langen Frontlinie zwischen Aserbaidschan und den be-

08

AZERBAIJAN

WEAPONS AND
WRATHFUL HEARTS

We make a gradual approach towards a place of fragility. Riding in an all-terrain vehicle belonging to the Army, we travel in the direction of the "Line of Contact" in Fizuli Rayon. "Line of Contact" is another name for the ceasefire line separating the positions held by the Azerbaijani Army and the Armenian separatists. On 12 May 1994, a ceasefire agreement between Armenia and Azerbaijan was signed. Prior to this, in the Fizuli area at least, the Azerbaijani Army managed to drive the separatists a certain distance back. This also explains why we have seen the ruins of houses during our drive. Here, battle once raged.

Lieutenant Colonel Sarvar Jebrailov tells us that shots are exchanged time and time again at the front line. The Armenian snipers are most active between midnight and 5am. "They are spontaneous shooting sprees without any specific target. It's a typical Soviet tactic used to keep up soldiers' morale," he adds. "Provocation." On the road to the foremost trench we make a stop at a tank depot, located a few kilometres from the Line of Contact. The T-72s are well camouflaged, sitting slightly sunken into the ground. Young soldiers are practising with one of the machines and want to demonstrate its flexibility to us on a test drive. "These are the best tanks," remarks an officer proudly. Artillery is another strong point in Azerbaijan's military capacity. There are observation posts installed around this area and it looks as if the army has settled in for a long stay, for eternity perhaps.

At one end of the trench there is a small building serving as accommodation for the troops. It is a stable concrete construction with a sparsely furnished dormitory. At this point, the soldiers are only about 200 metres from the lines of the opposing separatists. In between is the ceasefire line. The young soldiers walk with sure steps through the trench, which is about two metres deep. Through a small slit in a firing point, you can see the occupied land on the other side. Very near to the front line and immediately next to an Armenian armed post, ruined houses are to be seen. No one has lived in these buildings for a long time. The Azerbaijanis who once dwelled in these now destroyed and abandoned villages now live in refugee settlements.

Flight as a child, now in the army

"We can not forget what they have done to us. How could we ever live together with people who killed our relatives? I don't want that," says Samir Aliyev with vigour. The 23-year-old belongs to a small troop which serves in this foremost trench, a far-flung post on the front, for two weeks at a time. Samir Aliyev is different from his messmates in that he is himself a refugee from the area now occupied by Armenia. When he was only five years old, Aliyev was forced to flee Lachin with his family. Lachin, that hilly region with green valley floors and clear water running in the brooks and streams, is a very different scene from the dry, desert-like stretches of Azerbaijan where the refugees typically live, eking out a miserable existence in bland settlements or impoverished villages. On the night between 16 and 17 May 1992, the region fell into the hands of the Armenians. "I no longer remember fleeing, but I remember our house next to the mosque and the nature. I remember the children, the people." In Aliyev's family they still speak frequently about their previous life in the lost homeland. "If you try to keep your feelings bottled inside, they will burst out at some point anyway," the young man muses.

Along the approximately 120-kilometre-long front line between Azerbaijan and the occupied territories – and on the border between Ar-

setzten Gebieten, aber auch an der Grenze zwischen Armenien und Aserbaidschan nördlich Bergkarabachs, bei Schusswechseln durch Scharfschützen Soldaten und Zivilisten ums Leben. Alleine 2010 waren es offiziell rund 30 Tote. Jeweils beide Seiten machen jeweils die Gegenseite für die Verletzung des Waffenstillstandes verantwortlich. Auch über größere Vorfälle wird berichtet: Im Juni 2012 behaupteten die Armenier, dass eine 15 bis 20 Mann starke Einheit von aserbaidschanischen Soldaten armenische Positionen bei Tavush infiltriert hätte. Im September 2010 klagte Aserbaidschan, dass armenische Truppen die Waffenstillstandslinie überquert hätten.

Für Samir Aliyev ist der Dienst im vordersten Schützengraben aber auf jeden Fall Ehrensache. Er verzieht keine Miene während des Gesprächs. Er blickt dem Gegenüber auch nicht in die Augen. Seine Stimme, zu Beginn noch leicht stotternd, ist jetzt gefestigt. „Ich würde mein Leben geben für die Befreiung des Landes", sagt er. Das Heimweh der Entwurzelten ist groß.

Einigen ist der Geduldsfaden nach den vielen Jahren und den ergebnislosen Verhandlungen gerissen. Etwa den Mitgliedern der in der Hauptstadt Baku ansässigen Qarabag Azadlıq T skilatı (Organization of Karabakh Liberation, kurz KLO). Im Jahr 2000 wurde die Vereinigung als Nachfolgerin gleich ausgerichteter Gruppierungen gegründet. Die Büros der aus radikal eingestellten Flüchtlingen und deren Sympathisanten bestehenden Organisation sind nur über einen unscheinbaren Hinterhof zu erreichen. Die Räumlichkeiten der KLO sind nicht sehr groß, aber hier entwickeln die Mitglieder immer wieder Aktivitäten. Auch Publikationen gibt die KLO heraus. Die Berührungspunkte zwischen Armenien und Aserbaidschan sind nicht sehr vielfältig. Kommen jedoch im Rahmen von internationalen Treffen Delegierte oder für Sportveranstaltungen Athleten aus dem verfeindeten Nachbarland nach Baku, ist die KLO vor Ort und protestiert vehement.

Die Organisation ist in Unterverbände aufgeteilt, und nach eigenen Angaben hat sie mehrere Tausend Mitglieder. Während der Besuche bei Akif Nagi und seinen Mitstreitern wird bald klar, dass einige aus der zerstörten Stadt Agdam stammen. Die Flüchtlinge erzählen vom Kriegsausbruch, Gräueltaten der armenischen Besatzer und der Flucht. Gultekin Gulieva erinnert sich, wie zerstückelte Körper in Taschen von den Feinden zurückgegeben, wie zehn Frauen bei lebendigem Leib begraben wurden. „Als Mutter möchte man keinen Krieg, aber die Armenier erlaubten sich zu viel, ohne Krieg geht es wohl nicht, es braucht eine Revanche", sagt sie im Kreise ihrer Gesinnungsgenossen. Firudin Mamedov beispielsweise, hat seinerseits als Freiwilliger in einem Bataillon in der Region um Agdam und Agdere gekämpft. 1991 hätten die Armenier eine Zusammenkunft von Zivilisten in Agdam auf dem Zentralplatz mit Katjuscha-Raketen beschossen. Er habe selber gesehen, wie Menschen umkamen. Bis 1994 seien in der Gegend etwa 6000 Häuser bombardiert worden, erzählt er. Mamedov präsidiert heute in der KLO die Vereinigung der Kriegsinvaliden; im Kampf um Agdere hat er ein Auge verloren, auf dem anderen sieht er nur noch 40 Prozent. Der 29-jährige Elnur Guliev wiederum ist Vorsitzender der jungen Mitglieder. Als 11-Jähriger musste er die Stadt Agdam verlassen. Will die heutige Generation der jungen Aserbaidschaner denn überhaupt noch etwas mit diesem Konflikt zu tun haben? „Jetzt haben wir viele Mitglieder, die gar nicht aus Bergkarabach sind. Generell sind die Jungen bereit zu kämpfen, und sie wollen unser Land befreien", erklärt Elnur Guliev.

Da die seit dem Waffenstillstand von 1994 geführten Verhandlungen zwischen Armenien und Aserbaidschan bisher zu keinen konkreten Resultaten geführt haben, fordert KLO-Präsident Akif Nagi konkrete Schritte. „Es fanden viele Treffen zwischen den Präsidenten und mit der OSZE statt, aber es gab keine Ergebnisse. Das ist kein Weg. Die OSZE arbeitet sehr schlecht. Die Armenier wollen keine Resultate, sie machen, was sie wollen." Akif Nagis Position und die seiner Organisation ist klar. „Der einzige Weg ist die militärische Lösung."

menia and Azerbaijan north of Nagorno-Karabakh as well – soldiers and civilians are killed, over and over again, due to sniper gunfire. In 2010 alone the official death toll numbered 30. In each case, both sides blame their counterparts for having broken the ceasefire. The more important incidents are reported: in June 2012, for instance, the Armenians complained that a unit of Azerbaijani soldiers around 15-20 men strong had infiltrated Armenian positions in Tavush. In September 2010 Azerbaijan accused Armenian troops of having crossed the ceasefire line. For Samir Aliyev, serving in the foremost trench is a matter of honour. He maintains a steady countenance throughout our discussion. He doesn't look his interlocutor in the eye. At first he speaks with a slight stutter, then his voice becomes firm. "I would give my life for the liberation of the country," he says. The longing for home among the uprooted is yet strong.

After so many years of endless, unsuccessful negotiations, the patience of some is wearing thin. This applies to the members, for instance, of the Qarabağ Azadlıq Təşkilatı (Karabakh Liberation Organisation, or KLO for short), based in the capital Baku. This coalition was established in the year 2000 as the successor to a number of diverse groups with similar political alignments. The group is composed of refugees holding radical views and their sympathisers, but the offices it operates from are inconspicuous, accessible only via an unremarkable back courtyard. The KLO's premises are not large, but it is here that the members devise all sorts of activities. The KLO even issues publications. Points of contact between Armenians and Azerbaijanis are admittedly few and far between, but whenever visitors from the neighbouring enemy country come to Baku – delegates to international conferences or athletes for sporting events – the KLO is certain to be found on-site, protesting vehemently.

The organisation is divided into sub-groups and according to its own statements, numbers several thousand members. During my visits to Akif Nagi and his fellow campaigners, it soon became clear that some of them came from the destroyed city Agdam. The refugees spoke of the outbreak of war, of atrocities committed by the Armenian occupiers and of their eventual flight. Gultekin Gulieva remembers the enemies handing back bags of dismembered bodies, how ten women were buried alive. "As a mother you want no war, but the Armenians get away with too much. Without war, it just won't work. We need revenge," she says, within the circle of her like-minded comrades. Firudin Mamedov, for his part, fought in a battalion as a volunteer in the region around Agdam and Agdere. In 1991, he says, the Armenians opened fire on civilians gathered at Agdam's central square with Katyusha rockets. He saw himself how people died. By 1994, around 6,000 houses in the area had been bombarded. Mamedov now presides over the association of disabled war veterans within the KLO; he himself lost one eye in the battle of Agdere and has only about 40 percent vision in the other. Then there is 29-year-old Elnur Guliev, president of the youth members. He had to flee the city of Agdam when he was just 11. Does the current generation of young Azerbaijanis want to have anything to do with this conflict at all? "Today we have many members who aren't even from Nagorno-Karabakh. In general, the young people are ready to fight and want to liberate our country," Guliev answers.

Given that negotiations have been taking place between Armenia and Azerbaijan since the ceasefire in 1994 and that none of them have led to any tangible outcomes, KLO president Akif Nagi is demanding concrete steps be taken. "There have been numerous meetings between our President and the OSCE, but there have been no results. That is not a path leading anywhere. The OSCE works very poorly. The Armenians don't want results. They just do as they please." The position of Akif Nagi and his organisation is clear. "The only way forward is the military solution." They aren't against Armenians in general, they maintain, simply against the occupiers. Nagi explains that the KLO's aim is to urge the population to exert pressure on the government. The influence of the group so far, however, is marginal. Akif Nagi is familiar with the general geopolitical climate and knows that the international community and its organisations want to

Vorderster aserbaidschanischer Schützengraben,
Rayon Fizuli (März 2011)

Foremost trench of the Azerbaijan Army,
Fizuli Rayon (March 2011)

Man sei aber nicht gegen Armenien im Allgemeinen, sondern gegen die Besatzer. Nagi sagt, das Ziel der KLO sei es, die Bevölkerung dazu zu bringen, auf die Regierung Druck auszuüben. Doch der Einfluss der Gruppe ist bisher marginal. Akif Nagi kennt die geopolitische Großwetterlage und weiß, dass die internationale Gemeinschaft und ihre Organisationen Aserbaidschan an einem Krieg zu hindern versuchen. Bisher beschränkte sich Aserbaidschan denn auch auf das Aufrüsten seiner Armee und das gelegentliche Ausstossen von Kriegsrhetorik. „Wenn die Regierung genügend starkem Druck ausgesetzt und das Militär bereit ist, kann es losgehen", meint dagegen Akif Nagi.

prevent Azerbaijan from going to war. Up until now, Azerbaijan has limited itself to upgrading its army's capabilities and to the occasional outburst of war rhetoric. Nagi contends, nonetheless, "When the government is subject to strong enough pressure and when the military is ready, then it can start."

Diensttuender Trupp in vorderstem Schützengraben,
Rayon Fizuli (März 2011)

Azerbaijani unit on duty in the foremost trench,
Fizuli Rayon (March 2011)

Aserbaidschans Zaur Valiev, Samir Aliyev und Shaiq Maliyev
(von links) leisten ihren Dienst an der Waffenstillstandslinie.
Samir Aliyev stammt aus dem besetzten Lachin,
Rayon Fizuli (März 2011)

Azerbaijan's Zaur Valiev, Samir Aliyev and Shaiq Maliyev
(left to right) in active service at the ceasefire line. Samir Aliyev
is originally from the occupied Lachin region,
Fizuli Rayon (March 2011)

*Blick aus aserbaidschanischem Beobachtungsposten
auf die armenisch besetzte Seite,
Rayon Fizuli (März 2011)*

*View from the Azerbaijani Army's foremost trench, looking
towards the Armenian-occupied territories,
Fizuli Rayon (March 2011)*

*Diensttuende Soldaten der aserbaidschanischen
Armee an der Waffenstillstandslinie,
Rayon Fizuli (Oktober 2012)*

*Azerbaijani Army soldier on duty at the ceasefire line,
Fizuli Rayon (October 2012)*

*Blick aus dem aserbaidschanischen
Schützengraben auf ehemalige Weintanks,
Rayon Fizuli (Oktober 2012)*

*View from an Azerbaijani Army trench of damaged
wine tanks on the occupied side,
Fizuli Rayon (October 2012)*

*Diensttuende Soldaten der aserbaidschanischen
Armee an der Waffenstillstandslinie,
Rayon Fizuli (Oktober 2012)*

*Azerbaijani Army soldier on duty at the ceasefire line,
Fizuli Rayon (October 2012)*

Aserbaidschanischer Schützengraben,
Rayon Fizuli (Oktober 2012)

Azerbaijani trench,
Fizuli Rayon (October 2012)

Aufklärungsposten der aserbaidschanischen Armee,
Rayon Fizuli (März 2011)

Azerbaijani Army observation post,
Fizuli Rayon (March 2011)

Aserbaidschanische Aufklärung nahe der Waffenstillstandslinie,
Rayon Fizuli (März 2011)

Azerbaijani reconnaissance near the ceasefire line,
Fizuli Rayon (March 2011)

*Artillerieposition der aserbaidschanischen Armee nahe
der Waffenstillstandslinie,
Rayon Fizuli (März 2011)*

*Azerbaijani Army artillery post
near the ceasefire line,
Fizuli Rayon (March 2011)*

Artilleriepositionen der aserbaidschanischen
Armee nahe der Waffenstillstandslinie,
Rayon Fizuli (März 2011)

Azerbaijani Army artillery posts near
the ceasefire line,
Fizuli Rayon (March 2011)

*Wenige Kilometer von der Waffenstillstandslinie entfernt hat die
aserbaidschanische Armee eine Einheit Panzer stationiert,
Rayon Fizuli (März 2011)*

*A few kilometres behind the ceasefire line, the Azerbaijani
Army has stationed a unit of tanks,
Fizuli Rayon (March 2011)*

Denkmal beim strategischen Punkt Daslitepe,
Rayon Aghjabedi (Oktober 2012)

Monument at the strategic point Daslitepe,
Agdjabedi Rayon (October 2012)

09

WEDER KRIEG NOCH FRIEDEN

Auf den ersten Blick unterscheidet sich Tapqaraqoyunlu nicht von anderen Dörfern Aserbaidschans. Gänse watscheln über die Straße, in den Gärten gedeihen Granatäpfel. Die Straßen sind holprig und ungeteert. Auf dem Dorfplatz treffen sich ein paar Männer. Doch das Leben hier ist alles andere als normal. Es ist sehr gefährlich. Tapqaraqoyunlu im Distrikt Goranboy liegt direkt an der Waffenstillstandslinie des Krieges um Bergkarabach. Immer wieder geraten das Dorf und die dort lebenden Zivilisten unter Beschuss von armenischen Frontsoldaten. Von einem Waffenstillstand, der seit 1994 offiziell zwischen Armenien und Aserbaidschan herrschen soll, kann hier keine Rede sein. Die Fahne Aserbaidschans beim Dorfeingang ist eingezogen worden. Man will schließlich nicht provozieren. Für den Fall aller Fälle ist man aber gewappnet: Unauffällig ist eine Artilleriestellung der aserbaidschanischen Armee in der Nähe des Dorfes stationiert.

Die Wohngebäude, die sich im 2626 Einwohner zählenden Tapqaraqoyunlu exponiert und nahe von armenischen Positionen befinden, sind besonders in Gefahr. So wie das Haus von Kamil Allahverdiyev. Es liegt etwa 150 Meter Luftlinie von einem armenischen Wachtposten entfernt, der sich gegenüber auf einem Hügel befindet. Man erreicht Allahverdiyevs Zuhause nur über eine zwischen zwei Liegenschaften befindliche Straße, die wie auf dem Präsentierteller ungeschützt liegt, weshalb der Fahrer die kurze Strecke mit freier Sicht auf den Wachtposten rasend schnell zurücklegt. Das Leben hier

sei sehr schwierig und gefährlich, erzählt Kamil Allahverdiyev. Er zeigt Einschusslöcher an Dach und Wand; eine Mauer vor dem Haus hat er erhöht. „Jede Nacht sind wir in Angst", sagt der 34-jährige Bauer. Dann kommt seine Mutter hinzu, zeigt Rezepte für Medikamente, die sie nach jedem Beschuss der Armenier aus psychologischen Gründen zu sich nehme. „Seit ich in die 7. Klasse ging, schießen sie gelegentlich. Ich kenne den Grund nicht", so Kamil Allahverdiyev. Er kennt kein anderes Leben: Zuerst der Krieg und jetzt, seit 1994, permanente Gefahr. Der Bauer pflanzt Birnen, Äpfel, Weintrauben und Nüsse an, auf der gefährdeten Seite hinter dem Haus gedeihen Granatäpfel. Die aserbaidschanische Regierung habe zwar anderes Land angeboten, dieses sei aber für Landwirtschaft unbrauchbar, meint Allahverdiyev. Ein Wegzug aus dem Dorf kommt für ihn nicht infrage. „Das hier ist unser Land", bekräftigt er.

Nachts aufs Feld

Die Menschen haben sich mit den Begebenheiten arrangiert. Die Kinder kennen einen sicheren Weg zur Schule, der zwischen den Häusern hindurchführt. Rund ein Drittel der Dorfbewohner, also über 700, sind in der Landwirtschaft tätig. Viele gehen nur nachts auf die Felder zur Arbeit, weil sie tagsüber in Sichtweite der armenischen Soldaten sind. Wenn der Beschuss beginnt, wissen sich die Dorfbewohner zu helfen. Unter den Häusern befinden sich Schutzräume, wo sie sich verstecken können. Der Beschuss findet nur sporadisch statt, es gibt kein klares Zeitmuster, was die Lage für die Zivilisten umso unberechenbarer macht. Es kann auch vorkommen, dass die armenischen Soldaten vor der Wachstation sitzen und den ganzen Tag lang kein einziger Schuss abgegeben wird. Trotz aller Vorsicht wurde Allahverdiyevs Nachbar 2009 tödlich getroffen. Die Stelle, an der es geschah, liegt am Ende eines engen Durchgangs, vorne ungeschützt in Schussweite für die Armenier. „Wir hatten sogar Schwierigkeiten, seinen Leichnam zu bergen", erinnert sich Kamil Allahverdiyev. Der letzte Tote aufgrund armenischen Beschusses auf Zivilisten wurde in Tapqaraqoyunlu am

09

NEITHER WAR NOR PEACE

At first sight there is little to distinguish Tapqaraqoyunlu from other villages in Azerbaijan. Geese waddle through the streets and pomegranates thrive in the gardens. The streets are rough and unsealed. A few men gather at the village square. Yet life here is anything but normal. It is in fact extremely dangerous. Tapqaraqoyunlu, in the Goranboy district, lies directly on the ceasefire line drawn at the close of the Nagorno-Karabakh War. The village and the civilians who live there come under fire from Armenian front-line soldiers on a regular basis. In this place one can hardly speak of a ceasefire, which has officially been in effect between Armenia and Azerbaijan since 1994. The Azerbaijani flag at the entrance to the town has been brought down; ultimately, the villagers want to avoid any kind of provocation. Should the need arise, however, they are prepared: not far from the village, the Azerbaijan Army has deployed an inobtrusive artillery post.

The residential buildings of Tapqaraqoyunlu, a town counting 2,626 residents, are in particular danger, in light of their exposed location near the Armenian positions. Kamil Allahverdiyev's house is a case in point. It lies about 150 metres as the crow flies from an Armenian sentry post situated on a hill opposite. Allahverdiyev's home can only be reached via a street running between two other properties, which lies exposed and unprotected in unobstructed view of the sentry post. Drivers on this street are sitting targets, which is why the short distance must be covered at breakneck speed. Life here is

very difficult and dangerous, Kamil Allahverdiyev tells us resignedly. He shows us bullet holes on the roof and wall; out the front of the house he has erected an additional wall, which affords limited protection. "Every night, we are afraid," the 34-year-old farmer admits. His mother joins in and shows us prescriptions for medicine she takes after every Armenian gunfire attack, for psychological reasons. "They have been shooting, on and off, ever since I was in the seventh form at school. I don't know the reason," Kamil Allahverdiyev says. He knows no other life: first the war and then, as of 1994, ever-present danger. He grows pears, apples, grapes and nuts. On the vulnerable side of the house, pomegranates flourish. Though the Azerbaijani government has offered them alternative land, it is unusable for farming. For Allahverdiyev, moving away from the village is out of the question. "This is our land, right here," he affirms.

Out to the field at night

The people here have adapted their lives to cope with the incidents. The children know a safe path to get to school, which leads between houses. About a third of the villagers, that is to say more than 700, work in agriculture. Many of them go out to the fields only at night, as they are within sight of the Armenians soldiers during the day. When the shooting starts, the villagers know how to look after themselves; under the houses are shelters where they can hide. The gunfire is sporadic, following no clear time pattern, which makes the situation all the more unpredictable for the civilians. Sometimes the Armenian soldiers simply sit in front of the guardhouse all day and no shots are fired at all.

Despite all precautions, Allahverdiyev's neighbour was fatally hit in 2009. He was shot at the end of a narrow passageway, unprotected at the front and within gunshot range of the Armenians. "We even had difficulty recovering his body," Kamil Allahverdiyev recalls. The most recent death due to Armenian gunfire on civilians was registered in Tapqaraqoyunlu on 25 April 2011. The victim's name is commemorated on a memorial wall in the town, along with those

25. April 2011 registriert. Sein Name findet sich neben all denen anderer Dorfbewohner, die im Krieg oder nachher fielen, an einer Gedenkwand wieder. Dorfvorsteher Abbas Allahverdiyev erzählt, dass die Beerdigungen, entgegen dem muslimischen Ritus, dass der Tote noch vor dem Sonnenuntergang seine letzte Ruhe finden soll, nur nachts stattfinden können. Größere Menschenansammlungen sind gefährlich und könnten provozieren. Allahverdiyev zeigt den Friedhof: Dieser liegt am Ende des Dorfes, vor ihm befindet sich ein Schützengraben der aserbaidschanischen Armee.

Der kleine Fluss Inca versorgt Tapqaraqoyunlu mit Wasser. Doch etwa sechs Kilometer von der Ortschaft entfernt blockieren die Armenier häufig das Wasser. Eine Art Reservoir liegt zwischen den beiden gegnerischen Linien. Immer wieder zieht deshalb eine Gruppe von etwa 20 Männern nachts los, um die Blockade aufzuheben. Schaffen es die Männer vor Tagesanbruch nicht zurück, müssen sie sich stundenlang zwischen den Fronten verschanzen, bis es wieder dunkel wird. Erst jetzt, viele Jahre nach dem Krieg, gibt es laut Dorfvorsteher Abbas Allahverdiyev Pläne der aserbaidschanischen Regierung, eine 20 Kilometer lange Wasserleitung für die Versorgung der exponierten Ortschaft zu schaffen. Gelegentlich statten Beobachter der OSZE dem Dorf Tapqaraqoyunlu im Rahmen der Überwachung der Waffenstillstandslinie einen Besuch ab. Auch die armenischen Besatzer jenseits der Frontlinie werden darüber informiert, worauf während der Visite natürlich kein Schuss fällt. „Nachdem die Beobachter gegangen sind, ist dann dafür der Beschuss jeweils besonders heftig", sagt Bauer Kamil Allahverdiyev. Man fühlt sich hier von der zahnlos agierenden OSZE nicht erhört und nicht wahrgenommen.

Danach fahren wir nach Gapanly, einer Siedlung im Bezirk Terter. Diese befindet sich ebenfalls direkt an der Waffenstillstandslinie. Hier ist die Topografie anders beschaffen, ganz flach. Noch zu Kriegszeiten haben die Aserbaidschaner einen etwa fünf Kilometer langen und etwa drei Meter hohen Wall aus Erde gebaut, der die Siedlung um-

gibt und vor gegnerischem Beschuss schützen soll. Am Rande dieser Ortschaft befindet sich das Anwesen von Elkhan Tariverdiyev, ein paar Meter davor die dammähnliche Aufschüttung. Trotzdem haben es die Armenier geschafft, sein Haus zu beschießen. 2003 starb sein Vater durch den Schuss eines Scharfschützen. Nun ist Tariverdiyev gerade daran, eine zusätzliche Mauer vor seinem Haus zu bauen. Seine Frau hilft ihm bei der Zubereitung des Betons. Sein Nachbar Ali Aliyev erklärt derweil bei einem benachbarten Beobachtungsposten der aserbaidschanischen Armee die Ursache des Problems: Ein Blick auf die gegnerischen Linien zeigt, dass der Schützenstand der Armenier perfiderweise auf einem wohl extra aufgeschütteten Hügel gebaut worden ist. Zwar ist die aserbaidschanische Armee in der Gegend stationiert und gelegentlich sind Soldaten zu sehen. Die Präsenz ist aber unauffällig gehalten. „Wir hoffen, die Welt hört von unseren Lebensumständen und löst das Problem", sagt Ali Aliyev.

In der Stadt Terter erzählt Vivadi Baylarov, Vizegouverneur des Distriks, von weiteren Schwierigkeiten der Dörfer an der Waffenstillstandslinie. Die drei Flüsse Terter, Xacin und Inca, welche in den besetzten Gebieten entspringen und nach Aserbaidschan fließen, werden von den Separatisten gestaut, so Baylarov. Manchmal würden Minen mit dem Wasser mitgeschwemmt, die die Minenräumungsorganisation ANAMA dann entschärfen muss. Wenn die Armenier Chemikalien ins Wasser kippen und es dann von aserbaidschanischen Bauern zum Bewässern benutzt werde, seien die Felder danach für zehn Jahre unfruchtbar, berichtet Baylarov. Schüsse von gegenüber entfachen zudem Feuer auf den Feldern, 15 000 Hektaren seien so schon abgebrannt. In der Woche zuvor sei im Bezirk ein Bauer vom Schuss eines Scharfschützen verletzt worden. Während des Kriegs wurde bis vor die Stadt Terter gekämpft und gegen ein Dutzend Dörfer waren kurzzeitig besetzt – heute sind in der Gegend nach wie vor etwa 25 Hektare Land vermint. „Trotz dieser Umstände ist die Bevölkerung mutig und arbeitet weiter", sagt Vivadi Baylarov.

of all the other villagers who fell during or after the war. Village president Abbas Allahverdiyev tells us how the burial could not take place according to Muslim ordinance, which requires that the deceased person be laid to rest before sundown. In this case it could only take place at night, as large congregations of people are dangerous and could provoke the enemy. Abbas Allahverdiyev shows us the cemetery, which is located at the end of the village; in front of it is an Azerbaijani Army trench.

The small river Inca supplies Tapqaraqoyunlu with water but about six kilometres upstream from the village, the Armenians frequently block off the flow. Between the two enemy lines lies a kind of reservoir. Over and over again, a group of around 20 men must set off at night to remove the blockade. If they fail to return before daybreak they must dig themselves in between the front lines and wait until dark falls again. According to village president Abbas Allahverdiyev, the Azerbaijani government only now, many years after the war, has plans for a 20-kilometre-long water conduit to provide the exposed town with mains water. Now and again, observers from the OSCE pay a visit to the town of Tapqaraqoyunlu as part of the monitoring of the ceasefire line. The Armenian occupiers on the other side of the front line are informed of the visits too, which means of course that no shots are fired for the duration of each visit. "Once the observers have left, the shooting is consequently particularly heavy, every time," farmer Kamil Allahverdiyev says. The locals feel they are not heard or noticed by the OSCE, which itself is essentially toothless, or so it is perceived here.

Later we drive to Gapanly, a settlement in the Tartar district which, like Tapqaraqoyunlu, is located directly opposite the ceasefire line. The topography is quite different here, uniformly flat. During the war, the Azerbaijanis built a wall around the settlement. Made of earth, 5 kilometres long and 3 metres high, it was meant to protect the village from enemy firing. On the edge of this village lies Elkhan Tariverdiyev's property, and in front of it the embankment-like earth deposit.

In spite of it, the Armenians have still managed to shot at his house. In 2003, his father died at the hands of a sniper. Now Tariverdiyev has already started to build an additional wall in front of his house. His wife helps him with the preparation of the concrete. In the meantime, his neighbour Ali Aliyev points out the root of the problem from a neighbouring observation post belonging to the Azerbaijani army: a glance at the opposing force's lines reveals that the Armenian gunner's station has been built on top of a raised earth mound. No doubt this has been done on purpose, with dire consequences for the Azerbaijani villagers. Although the Azerbaijani army is stationed in the area and its soldiers are sometimes to be seen, their presence remains low-key. "We hope that the world hears of our living conditions and solves the problem," is all Ali Aliyev has to say.

In the city of Tartar, district vice-governor Vivadi Baylarov tells of more difficulties for the villages lying on the ceasefire line. The separatists regularly dam up the three rivers Tartar, Xacin and Inca, which originate in the occupied territories and flow thenceforth into Azerbaijan, he says. Sometimes mines are washed down with the water, which must be deactivated by the mine-clearing organisation ANAMA. Worse still is when the Armenians tip chemicals into the water, which is then used for irrigation by the Azerbaijani farmers; this can render the fields sterile for up to ten years, Baylarov reports. Shelling from the opposite side can also spark fires in the fields, which has already caused 15,000 hectares to be burnt. Just last week a farmer in the area was injured by sharpshooter fire, he says. During the war, the fighting came right up to Tartar city and around a dozen villages were occupied for a short time. About 25 hectares of land in the local area were and still are mined. Undeterred, the people live with the danger. As Vivadi Baylarov tells us, "Despite these circumstances, the populace is brave and keeps on working."

Uninhabitable villages and settlements
The village Alkhanly in the Fizuli Rayon is divided in two. It is situated only a short distance from the ceasefire line and the inhabitants

Unbewohnbare Dörfer und Siedlungen

Das Dorf Alkhanli im Rayon Fizuli ist zweigeteilt. Nicht weit von der Waffenstillstandslinie entfernt, dürfen die Einwohnern nur in einem Bereich der Ortschaft wohnen. Ein Checkpoint der aserbaidschanischen Armee kontrolliert den Verkehr in dieses Niemandsland. Durch eine Lücke in der Wolkendecke dringen Sonnenstrahlen und fallen auf die ruinenübersäte Landschaft. Etwas weiter entfernt, vielleicht schon im armenisch besetzten Teil Fizulis, steigt eine helle Rauchsäule empor. Eine merkwürdige Atmosphäre liegt über dieser Region. Das gesamte Rayon ist zweigeteilt. Ein Teil Fizulis, darunter dessen frühere, gleichnamige Hauptstadt, ist nach wie vor unter Kontrolle der Separatisten. Immerhin 22 Dörfer konnten die Aserbaidschaner 1993 nach der kurzzeitigen Besetzung durch die Armenier wieder befreien. Dazu gehört auch die Ortschaft Asagi Abdurrahmanli. Doch aufgrund der ebenfalls topografisch speziellen Lage ist das gesamte Dorf verwaist. Von hier gibt es immer wieder Berichte über Schüsse von den benachbarten armenischen Positionen und auch während unseres Besuches der Ortschaft fällt einer. Die Folgen des Krieges sind auch hier allgegenwärtig: Häuserskelette. Das große Schulgebäude liegt teilweise in Trümmern, an der Decke im Erdgeschoss sind Brandspuren auszumachen.

Auch das Dorf Chirakli im unbesetzten Teil des Rayons Agdam ist zweigeteilt. Die Gegend ist flach; die Waffenstillstandslinie ist hier kein gerader Strich. Frontliniengräben zerfurchen das Land. Der Schutzwall, der die Einwohner gegen die armenischen Scharfschützen abschirmen soll, geht mitten durch das Dorf. Im nicht weit davon gelegenen Orta Qarvand wurde 2011 der neunjährige Fariz Badalov unweit seines Elternhauses von einer Kugel getroffen und starb. Nun wurde eine drei Meter hohe Mauer gebaut, die nun das Land der Badalovs umgibt. Der Friedhof, wo sich Fariz` Grab im vorderen Teil befindet, ist ebenfalls nur wenige hundert Meter von der Frontlinie entfernt. Wer in geduckter Haltung in den hinteren Teil des Friedhofs geht, sieht auch auf der Rückseite der neueren Grabsteine Einschusslöcher. Selbst der Gottesacker ist nicht vor armenischem Beschuss sicher. Unsere Fahrt durch die aserbaidschanischen Frontdörfer führt unter anderem weiter zur unterbrochenen Hauptverbindungsstraße von Barda nach Agdam, das sich jetzt in Schutt und Asche liegend im armenisch besetzten Teil Aserbaidschans befindet. Etwas außerhalb der Ortschaft Hüseynli gibt es eine Polizeisperre, die man noch passieren darf. Etwas später folgen ein Armeeposten und ein Stoppschild. Hinter dem Schlagbaum versperrt ein aufgeschütteter Erdwall die Weiterfahrt in die armenisch besetzten Gebiete Aserbaidschans.

Die tagelange Fahrt entlang der Waffenstillstandslinie offenbart noch einmal in aller Deutlichkeit die schrecklichen Folgen der armenischen Besetzung Bergkarabachs und der benachbarten Distrikte. Eine Politik der zerstörten Leben, der verbrannten Erde, der Entwurzelung Hunderttausender Aserbaidschaner. 20 Jahre nach dem Krieg lassen die Auswirkungen Menschen mit tiefen seelischen Wunden und in Armut zurück. Auf der Fahrt gab es Begegnungen mit vielen Menschen mit den unterschiedlichsten, berührenden Schicksalen. Die Frage zu ihrer Zukunft bleibt unbeantwortet. Oder was soll man dem alten Mann auf dem Bahngleis in Kücerli antworten, der in Tränen ausbricht, weil er nicht zurück in seine Heimat kann? Was soll man Ashig Akbar „Kelbecerli" Shirinov sagen, der in seinem erzwungenen Exil Barda das traditionelle Instrument Saz spielt und von der Schönheit seiner derzeit unerreichbaren, besetzten Heimat Kelbajar singt?

may only live in one part of the town. The Azerbaijani army controls traffic into the no-man's-land at a checkpoint. As I look out beyond it, rays of sunshine pierce through a gap in the blanket of clouds and illuminate the ruin-studded landscape. At a distance – perhaps already in the Armenian-held part of Fizuli – a column of pale-coloured smoke rises up in the air. A peculiar atmosphere hangs over this region. The entire rayon is split into two parts: one part of Fizuli is still under the control of the separatists, including the former capital of the same name. Nevertheless, 22 towns were returned to Azerbaijani control, freed by local forces in 1993 after a short-lived occupation by the Armenians. Ashagy Abdurakhmanly is one such village, yet the whole town lies deserted due to its particular topographic situation. There are still many reports of gunfire from the neighbouring Armenian position here, and during our visit to the town, yet another attack took place. As in other places, here too are those ubiquitous testaments to the legacy of war: the skeletal remains of houses. The large schoolhouse lies half in rubble, and we can see that the ground floor ceiling is marked by fire.

The town of Chirakhly in the unoccupied part of Agdam Rayon is divided also. The local area is flat and the ceasefire line here is neither straight nor simple; the countryside is furrowed by front line trenches. The protective wall built to shield the inhabitants from Armenian sharpshooters runs right through the middle of the town. Not far from here in the village of Orta-Karvend, nine-year-old resident Fariz Badalov was shot dead while playing near his parents' house in 2011. Since then, a wall three metres high has been built around the Badalovs' land. Young Fariz's grave can be found towards the front of a cemetery only a few hundred metres from the front line. To visit the back of the cemetery, one must crouch down for safety; there are bullet holes to be seen in the back of the newer gravestones. Even the graveyard is not safe from Armenian fire.

Our travels through the Azerbaijani villages at the front lead us at one point to the main connecting highway – now interrupted – running from Barda to Agdam, the city which now lies in rubble and ashes in the Armenian-held part of Azerbaijan. A little outside of the town of Hüseynli is a police roadblock through which one may still pass. Somewhat further along there is an army post and a stop sign. Behind the turnpike, a raised embankment of earth definitively bars any further passage into Azerbaijan's occupied territories.

The several-day journey along the ceasefire line reveals once more in all clarity the terrible consequences of the Armenian occupation of Nagorno-Karabakh and the neighbouring districts. It has been a policy of scorched earth and ruined lives, the uprooting of hundreds of thousands of Azerbaijanis. Twenty years after the war, the repercussions include a trail of people with deep psychological wounds, left in poverty. Throughout my travels I met many people whose fates and fortunes were widely varied, yet all had moving stories to tell. The question of their future remains unanswered. Yet what should one say to the wizened old man on the railway tracks in Kyucharli who bursts into tears because he can't return home? What should one say to Ashig Akbar "Kelbecerli" Shirinov, who lives in forced exile in Barda, plays his traditional instrument, the Saz, and sings of the beauty of his currently inaccessible, occupied homeland Kalbajar?

Denkmal für die Gefallenen in Tapqaraqoyunlu. Die letzten Opfer wegen des Konflikts – notabene Zivilisten – gab es in den Jahren 2009 und 2011 – gestorben an Schüssen von benachbarten armenischen Positionen, Rayon Goranboy (Oktober 2011)

Monument to the Fallen at Tapqaraqoyunlu, Azerbaijan. The most recent victims of the conflict – civilians, notably – lost their lives in 2009 and 2011, shot dead by Armenian snipers, Goranboy Rayon (October 2011)

*Armenische Position auf der besetzten Seite, gesehen
vom aserbaidschanischen Dorf Tapqaraqoyunlu aus,
Rayon Goranboy (Oktober 2011)*

*Armenian post on the occupied side, seen from the
Azerbaijani village Tapqaraqoyunlu,
Goranboy Rayon (October 2011)*

Muhardiz Ismailov bei seinem Haus. Das Fenster hat er aus Sicherheitsgründen gegen armenischen Beschuss zugemauert, Tapqaraqoyunlu, Rayon Goranboy (Oktober 2011)

Muhardiz Ismailov in front of his home. He has bricked up the window for safety because of gunfire from the Armenian side, Tapqaraqoyunlu, Goranboy Rayon (October 2011)

Dorfbewohner Kamil Allahverdiyev vor einer zusätzlichen, hohen Mauer, die vor armenischem Beschuss schützen soll, Tapqaraqoyunlu, Rayon Goranboy (Oktober 2011)

Villager Kamil Allahverdiyev in front of an additional wall which has been erected to protect from Armenian gunfire, Tapqaraqoyunlu, Goranboy Rayon (October 2011)

*Bewohner aus Gapanly bei einem um das Dorf aufgeschütteten
Damm, der vor armenischem Beschuss schützen soll,
Rayon Terter (Oktober 2011)*

*Villagers of Gapanly near an embankment which was erected
around the settlement to protect from Armenian gunfire,
Terter Rayon (October 2011)*

Elkhan Tariverdiyev baut eine Mauer um sein Grundstück, der
aufgeschüttete Wall ums Dorf sorgt nicht mehr für genügend Schutz,
Gapanly, Rayon Terter (Oktober 2011)

Elkhan Tariverdiyev is building a wall around his property, as the
elevated wall surrounding the village does not afford enough protection,
Gapanly, Rayon Terter (October 2011)

Kurzzeitig armenisch besetztes Dorf Alkhanli,
Fizuli Rayon, Aserbaidschan (Oktober 2012)

The village Alkhanly was for a short time under Armenian occupation,
Fizuli Rayon, Azerbaijan (October 2012)

Kurzzeitig armenisch besetztes Dorf Alkhanli,
Fizuli Rayon, Aserbaidschan (Oktober 2012)

The briefly Armenian-occupied village Alkhanly,
Fizuli Rayon, Azerbaijan (October 2012)

Kurzzeitig armenisch besetztes Dorf Ashagi Abdurrahmanli,
Rayon Fizuli, Aserbaidschan (Oktober 2012)

The briefly Armenian-occupied village Ashagy Abdurrakhmanly,
Fizuli Rayon, Azerbaijan (October 2012)

Kurzzeitig armenisch besetztes Dorf Ashagi Abdurrahmanli,
Rayon Fizuli, Aserbaidschan (Oktober 2012)

The briefly Armenian-occupied village Ashagy Abdurrakhmanly,
Fizuli Rayon, Azerbaijan (October 2012)

Kurzzeitig armenisch besetztes Dorf Ashagi Abdurrahmanli,
Rayon Fizuli, Aserbaidschan (Oktober 2012)

The briefly Armenian-occupied village Ashagy Abdurrakhmanly,
Fizuli Rayon, Azerbaijan (October 2012)

Kurzzeitig armenisch besetztes Dorf Ashagi Abdurahmanli,
Rayon Fizuli, Aserbaidschan (Oktober 2012)

The briefly Armenian-occupied village Ashagy Abdurakhmanly,
Fizuli Rayon, Azerbaijan (October 2012)

Kurzzeitig armenisch besetztes Dorf Ashagi Abdurrahmanli,
Rayon Fizuli, Aserbaidschan (Oktober 2012)

The briefly Armenian-occupied village Ashagy Abdurrakhmanly,
Fizuli Rayon, Azerbaijan (October 2012)

An der Waffenstillstandslinie bei Chirakli,
Rayon Agdam (Oktober 2012)

Near the ceasefire line at Chirakly,
Agdam Rayon (October 2012)

Schutzwall vor armenischem Beschuss,
Chirakli, Rayon Agdam (Oktober 2012)

Protection embankment from Armenian gunfire,
Chirakli, Agdam Rayon (October 2012)

An der Waffenstillstandslinie bei Chirakli,
Rayon Agdam (Oktober 2012)

Near the ceasefire line at Chirakly,
Agdam Rayon (October 2012)

An der Waffenstillstandslinie bei Chirakli,
Rayon Agdam (Oktober 2012)

Near the ceasefire line at Chirakly,
Agdam Rayon (October 2012)

Siyavus Sukuzov mit Sohn Ibrahim vor ihrem beschossenem Wohnhaus an der Waffenstillstandslinie, Rayon Agdam (Oktober 2012)

Siyavuz Sukuzov with his son Ibrahim in front of their shelled house near the ceasefire line, Agdam Rayon (October 2012)

Blick Richtung besetztes Bas Qarvand vom Friedhof bei Chirakli, Rayon Agdam (Oktober 2012)

View of occupied Bas Qarvand from the cemetery near Chirakly, Agdam Rayon (October 2012)

Grab von Fariz Badalov auf dem Friedhof bei Chirakli. Der 9-jährige Junge wurde in Orta Qarvand an der Waffenstillstandslinie erschossen, Rayon Agdam (Oktober 2012)

Fariz Badalov's grave in the cemetery near Chirakly. The boy was shot dead in Orta-Karvend by an Armenian sniper, Agdam Rayon (October 2012)

Unterbrochene Straße Barda-Agdam bei Tazakand,
Rayon Terter (Oktober 2011)

Interrupted highway Barda-Agdam near Tazakand,
Tartar Rayon (October 2011)

Sicht Richtung Berge des besetzten Bergkarabach; bei Hasankaya und Maragha, Rayon Terter (Oktober 2012)

View from a former agricultural reserach institute near Gasankaya und Maragha, Tartar Rayon (October 2012)

QUELLENVERZEICHNIS

Alle Texte und Fotos (2008–2012) von André Widmer

Kapitel 1, 2, 4, 5, 6, 7, 8 und 9: Basierend auf Recherchen des Autors vor Ort in Bergkarabach und Aserbaidschan zwischen Mai 2008 und Oktober 2012. Teile der Kapitel erschienen als Reportagen in „Die Welt" (Deutschland), „Frankfurter Rundschau" (Deutschland), „Tages-Anzeiger" (Schweiz), „WOZ Die Wochenzeitung" (Schweiz), „Neues Deutschland" (Deutschland), „Moskauer Deutsche Zeitung" (Russland) und in den Onlinemedien „Neuland" (Schweiz) und „20 Minuten online" (Schweiz).

Kapitel 3: Basierend auf Recherchen des Autors vor Ort im März 2010. Geschichtliche Angaben aus dem Buch „War against Azerbaijan", Baku 2010.

Vorgeschichte, Eskalation, Krieg: Wikipedia; Heiko Langner: „Krisenzone Südkaukasus", Berlin 2009.

Politische Standpunkte: Basierend auf Gesprächen vor Ort zwischen Mai 2008 und März 2011, die Aussagen von Robert Avetisyan (Washington) per E-Mail am 15. April 2010.

SOURCE MATERIALS

All text and photographs (2008 – 2012) by André Widmer
Chapters 1, 2, 4, 5, 6, 7, 8 and 9: Based on the author's on-site research in Nagorno-Karabakh and Azerbaijan between May 2008 and October 2012.
Parts of these chapters appeared as reports in "Die Welt" (Germany), "Frankfurter Rundschau" (Germany), "Tages-Anzeiger" (Switzerland), "WOZ Die Wochen-zeitung" (Switzerland), "Neues Deutschland" (Germany), "Moskauer Deutsche Zeitung" (Russia) and in the online publications "Neuland" (Switzerland) and "20 Minuten online" (Switzerland).

Chapter 3: Based on the author's on-site research in March 2010, with historical information from "War against Azerbaijan", Baku 2010.

Background, Escalation, War: Wikipedia; Heiko Langner: "Krisenzone Südkaukasus, Köster, Berlin, 2009.

Political Standpoints: Based on on-site conversations between May 2008 and March 2011 and statements from Robert Avetisyan (Washington) by email on the 15 April 2010.

DANK

Ich möchte allen Menschen danken, die ich besuchen und befragen durfte, die mir ihre Haustüren geöffnet und ihre Erlebnisse und Lebensgeschichten erzählt haben. Ihnen gehört auch mein ganzer Respekt. Großen Dank auch allen Personen, die mir Termine und Besuche ermöglicht und gewährt und damit in irgendeiner Weise dazu beigetragen haben, dass ich vor Ort für meine Reportagen recherchieren konnte. In Aserbaidschan danke ich vor allem Ali Kadyrov, Anar Hidayatov, Goshgar Zeynalov und den regionalen Behörden für Mithilfe und Unterstützung als auch den lokalen Gastgebern; in Bergkarabach David Babayan für seine Mithilfe, in Deutschland Heiko Langner und Gayane Apinyan. Auch für die Gastfreundschaft allerorts sei hiermit gedankt. Die Mitarbeit verschiedener Fachpersonen in der Produktion (Namen siehe Impressum) hat es erst ermöglicht, das Buch in dieser Qualität erscheinen zu lassen. Auch ihnen vielen Dank.

Nicht vergessen auszusprechen möchte ich auch meine Dankbarkeit an jene, die mich zu meinem Buch ermutigt haben sowie an mein nahes persönliches Umfeld, Familie und Freunde.

DER AUTOR

André Widmer (geboren 1973, wohnhaft in Gränichen/Schweiz) ist Journalist. Seit 2006 verfasst er Reportagen über Themen aus den Ex-Sowjetrepubliken. Veröffentlicht wurden seine Texte unter anderem in der NZZ, der NZZ am Sonntag, der Frankfurter Allgemeinen Sonntagszeitung, der Welt, Tages-Anzeiger, Neues Deutschland und Die Wochenzeitung WOZ. Intensiv recherchiert hat er im Südkaukasus über den Konflikt um Bergkarabach.